Ecommerce

by

Matthew Scott

Amazon FBA:

Step by Step Guide on How to Make Money by Selling on Amazon

by

Matthew Scott

FREE BOOK

I have included this FREE book that will help you make money to help you out in many ways! Do you need funds for your ecommerce business or shopify store? Well grab this guide while you can.

HTTPS://ONLINEPGS.LPAGES.CO/MAKEMONEYONLINE

10 WAYS TO MAKE YOUR FIRST $100 ONLINE!

Table of Contents

Introduction

Amazon offers two ways for you to sell your products on their website. One involves handling everything yourself, including customer service, shipments, and almost every detail of the process. The other method involves having them handle everything from shipping, to customer service, to refunds and exchanges, and more. The second method is referred to as Fulfillment by Amazon, often abbreviated to simply FBA. There are many perks to both methods, but Fulfillment by Amazon is tailor made for those people that aren't simply selling a few items, don't own a warehouse, cannot or don't wish to hire a staff, don't want to constantly work on shipping out hundreds of small packages, and don't want the added headache of handling customer service. The added benefits of having Amazon (via Fulfillment by Amazon) handle a bulk of the work includes offering customers every possible perk available, such as free two-day shipping for Prime members, quality assurance, and excellent customer service from a provider that can be trusted.

While the path of selling in large quantities online is not always an easy one, it is a rewarding path to take. Not only is it a business where there's no true boss (unless you hire someone), but it is extremely scalable, doesn't require a lot of special skills, and doesn't involve the extremely steep startup costs that typical brick and mortar or dedicated retail website businesses incur. While it does require capital to purchase products, it doesn't required heavy marketing up front (more on this later), and it doesn't require you to be an expert salesperson. One of the best perks is that you can truly dip your toes in a bit before going into it fulltime. It can be handled as a second income stream that will grow and blossom into a main source of income. It can truly become your escape from the nine to five grind from there if you are dedicated to that goal.

The process is not painfully difficult, and once a seller gets the swing of things, the only issue limiting the potential profits is willingness to work hard and persistence. While the process itself is easy, you should not mistake this as easy money. This is not a get-rich-quick method, and if you're a serial entrepreneur you've probably learned that none of the promises involved with such schemes tend to pan out. While Amazon will fulfil the orders and handle the shipment and customer service, that doesn't mean you can afford to simply sit around. Quite the opposite is true. Instead, your time is freed up to continuously be on the lookout for new products that are worth selling, building your business, and for some, even time to create your own products and brands. This is how a one-person retail operation is possible: Amazon does a large number of the menial tasks for you so you can focus on finding the profitable products.

The journey can be a slow one, or it can be a fast one. It is entirely dependent on how much work, time, and energy is expended by the seller. The great thing is that almost ANYONE can be successful at it, and with a little bit of insider knowledge, you should have no problem getting started and learning the ropes. Taking your time to do some research now, you're setting yourself up to avoid some of the most obvious mistakes made by even the most successful FBA sellers in the business when they first strated, and for that I commend you greatly. Are you ready to get started?

Chapter 1. Setting Up a FBA Account

Setting up an Amazon Seller Central account to sell products online is the first step to creating a business around Fulfillment by Amazon. The process is fairly simple, but there are a few considerations that can make it easier and quicker.

Step 1. Gather Required Materials

Before you can begin setting up your Amazon Seller Central account, you'll need a handful of materials and information on hand. It is best to gather these items together now, or the process will take longer than necessary as you're hunting down each bit of information as you set up your account and your first shipment. The required materials include:

- An email address, ideally one specifically for your new business, but it can be your personal email address as well.
- A credit card or ATM card. Again, this can be dedicated to your new business venture, but it can also be your personal accounts. For reporting and tax purposes, having a separate account is extremely helpful in simplifying certain aspects of your business down the road.
- A physical address. In this case, your home address is perfectly fine. There's almost no reason to have a separate address.

- A social security number, which you probably know by heart.

- A phone number. Your personal phone is fine. Customers are not going to be calling this line, so it's mostly just for your communications with Amazon should anything need to be handled outside of email.

- A bank account and the bank's routing number. If you have a checkbook, this routing number is typically at the bottom of the checks. Otherwise, perform a quick Google search for "MYBANKNAME route number," and it should easily be found from there. You can also ask your bank teller for this information. Again, a separate account for your business can simplify some processes later on.

- An Amazon account, which you probably already have. Important: do NOT start multiple accounts, as this is a violation of their terms of service. The only exception is if you have a registered business.

Step 2. Sign Up for Amazon's Seller Central

Before you can opt into their Fulfillment by Amazon services, you'll need to begin with a simple Seller Central account.

In your web browser, navigate to https://sellercentral.amazon.com. You will be asked to log into your Amazon account. On this page, it might say that you don't currently have access to sell on Amazon, but there will be a button that says, "Register." Click this button, and you'll be taken to the next page.

Step 3. Choosing a Seller Account

The following page will prompt you to choose which type of seller account you want. The options are "professional" and "individual."

A professional account currently costs $40 per month, and for most of us it is going to be a huge asset. It comes with a wealth of perks, and any serious seller will eventually want to pony up for one. If you do hold off on this now, once you begin selling more than forty items, it's time to upgrade to the professional account. Perks of a professional account include:

- The $0.99 cent fee per sale no longer applies. This is why anyone selling over 40 items per month may as well sign up for the professional account. Anything after 40 items sold on a personal account is just throwing a dollar away after every sale. That can add up to serious losses quickly.

- With a professional account, additional data and analytics are available to you, including extra downloadable spreadsheets, inventory lists, and reports pertaining to sales and listings.

- Listing management becomes easier for multiple items at once thanks to advanced listing tools.

- Ability (but not guarantee) to have your product become the one that's placed in the cart from the "Buy Box." The buy box is the box to the right on product pages that can be clicked on to quickly go ahead and add the item to the cart without looking through other offers. This can be very competitive for popular items, but without a professional account, you have zero chance of obtaining this coveted benefit.

- More product categories are available to you than with the free account, expanding the types of products you are allowed to sell through Amazon. While some of the most obvious products people start selling don't apply here, it is still a huge perk once you move into those categories.

- Promotional codes and coupon codes can be generated to create incentive for buyers to purchase from you. This can be a huge marketing technique, so not having the ability to offer promotions like this can mean less sales overall.

To start with, it is fine to use a free account until you have enough sales to justify the $40 per month costs involved with a professional account. Enrollment in a professional account can be changed at any time, but just keep in mind that if you're taking advantage of any of the perks of a professional seller account, you'll lose these should you choose to switch back to an individual account. You are going to immediately enjoy the benefits of a professional account, though, so that isn't likely to be a concern unless you aren't selling anything.

Step 4. Fill in Personal Details

Once you've selected the seller account plan you desire, you'll be taken to a page asking for your business and personal information. Go ahead and fill this out.

For the name, you can put your personal name or the name of your business or LLC if it is registered.

At this stage, you will be asked to review the terms of agreement and accept them. Take time to understand these, and then proceed to the next page. While it is tempting to simply press, "I Agree," it could come back to haunt you in the future should you violate their terms.

Finally, we have a form for completing the registration process. This includes several parts:

- Display name – This is the name that customers see for your shop when they're looking at products you sell. You cannot use the same display name as other sellers, but you can change your display name as many times as you like. Use something professional. People are less interested in buying a book from, "KillXSwitchXPushed" than they are from "BooksAreLife."

- Business address – This will likely be your home address unless you happen to have a storefront or a warehouse, which is probably not the case.

- Main product category (optional) – Only choose a category here if there is a particular niche that you intend to sell in. For most people, it's fine to leave this blank. For people that are selling on Amazon because they've developed a product or brand, it may be worth setting a main product category.

- Number of products you plan on selling (optional) – This is an estimate. There's no need to fill it out.

- Are you the brand owner? (optional) – If you've created a brand yourself and this is the product or line of products you intend to sell through Fulfillment by Amazon, then you can answer this question. If you're not a brand creator/owner, don't worry about it. Don't worry, if you develop a product or brand later, nothing will stop you from being able to sell it just because you didn't answer this question.

The three optional questions can be left blank, and they can be changed at a later date if the situation you're in as a seller changes. If any information is attributed to these questions, be sure to alter them if anything changes or you take a new direction with your business.

Once you're done here, click "Save and Continue."

The following page will have you enter your credit card information. This credit card will be used to pay for your membership fees and any other fees not covered by your proceeds. (Fees will be covered in more depth later on.) Once you've completed this form, press "Save and Continue" again.

Next, Amazon will ask that you verify your identity. This is completed either through a phone call or through a text message. Both are quick and painless processes, so just choose whichever you prefer. Once you receive the call or text, type in the PIN number provided to verify your identity, and then click the "Continue" button.

The following page requests tax information. Enter these details and continue, and then your account is ready for business!

That's all there is to it. From here, we'll begin discussing what is required to begin selling.

Chapter 2: Getting Prepared to Sell

Amazon Seller Central is obviously in place for the sale of physical goods. Even if you're having Amazon fulfil your orders for you, it is required that you package, print labels, and ship your items to Amazon warehouses. The good news is that you'll be shipping several items per box rather than shipping everything individually whenever somebody places an order. As a result, the day-to-day work of fulfilling orders is off your hands, and it also means you can have more warehouse space than your spare bedroom allows. Unfortunately, unlike handling every part on your own, there are going to be slightly more upfront costs involved, which includes a little bit of risk. Don't let that deter you; the risk is much smaller than other business models. Once things are going smoothly, the investments will have been well worth it.

Part of those initial costs are all the items you'll require just to make shipments. While you may be able to struggle by without some of these, it is highly recommended to make the investment. These items include:

- A computer and internet access; hopefully you already have these at the ready.
- The Amazon Seller app for your Android or iOS smartphone. Using this to scan products and research is going to help you

stay on top of the game. This is a requirement. If you don't have a smart phone, you're years behind your competition, and you really need to buy one.

- A laser jet printer. Amazon requires laser printing instead of inkjet because inkjet has a bad habit of smudging, which causes problems when it's time to find your items in the warehouse. If you do use an inkjet printer, be sure to place clear shipping tape over all readable parts, barcodes, etc.

- Label paper or printer paper. Avery 5160 (30) sized label papers are the best for the job. You can technically do the job with plain paper, but you will save yourself a lot of time and headache just forking out for the label paper with adhesive backing. Alternatively, you can have Amazon label your products for you instead, but this incurs as $0.20 charge per product, which really cuts into your profits if you're not moving a large amount of product.

- Scissors. They just need to work! Nothing special there, and you probably have a decent pair already.

- Postal scale. Get a reliable one. Cheap postal scales are notorious for breaking quickly, giving false readouts, and causing headaches that end in returned packages. It must be able to accurately weigh your boxes up to 50 pounds as well, as this is the largest size box you can send to Amazon for fulfillment services and it is wise to fill boxes as much as possible. (In a pinch, you can always use the method of standing on a standard bathroom scale with the box in your arms and subtracting your weight from the readout. This method isn't as reliable, though, and you need to replace it with a decent postal scale as soon as possible.)

- Shipping tape. The "guns" are best, but whatever you're willing to work with will get the job done. Clear shipping tape is a must because it can be used to cover labels as well.

- Cleaning supplies, such as Goo Gone, Scotty Peelers, Magic Erasers, etc. Your items need to be cleaned before shipping. Do NOT sell dirty items.

- A barcode scanner is an optional asset that you should buy once you're serious about this business. This makes it incredibly simple to look up any items with a barcode on the fly, especially making the listing process quicker. You can simply type in the barcode when searching on Amazon instead, so this is really never REQUIRED, but it is highly recommended. Your Amazon Seller App does scan codes, but it does not automatically input them for you on any field forms during listing.

- Clear poly bags for smaller items (CDs, DVDs, toys). This is a smart move on your part, and Amazon often requires it anyway. The better you protect your items, the less likely you have to deal with the losses incurred by returns later.

- Bubble wrap, paper, or other padding to help protect your items during shipment. You cannot use any Styrofoam peanuts or similar items, as Amazon does not allow for them. If you must reuse your packing peanuts, you need to secure them in some type of bag first.

- Boxes, multiple sizes, to place all your items in. You want boxes that are good for individual items and boxes for shipping batches of products to Amazon. (Amazon will require some items to be placed in a box prior to being placed in the larger box of items.)

- Box cutter to resize boxes as needed, which is important for avoiding additional shipping charges. If you have a healthy stash of boxes, this may not be a big deal.

- A shoebox or filing cabinet to save all your receipts in. You'll be able to write this stuff off on your taxes, so don't lose track of money spent.

Once you have all your supplies ready, or while you're gathering them, it's time to start sourcing products to sell, which we'll need before going into detail about how to setup Fulfillment by Amazon.

Chapter 3. Sourcing Products

This is a key step in the process. Finding products for a price that allows room for profit is likely going to become the bulk of your workload as an Amazon FBA seller. There are many outlets for product sourcing or creation, and there are many names for this process, including retail arbitrage, junking, thrifting, scouting, picking, and reselling.

When looking for items to buy, it's important to remember the "buy low, sell high" rule. With Fulfillment by Amazon, a decent rule of thumb is that you should try to buy items that will sell for almost three times as much as you are paying for them. Because of fees, shipping, and other costs involved, going much lower than this may often be a waste of time and energy.

If you haven't yet, download the Amazon Seller app on your smartphone. This tool will greatly help in certain situations, and going without it is almost downright hurting yourself. While sourcing items, using this app to scan the barcode will show you the prices and product details on Amazon. You can also pay attention to the other people selling the product. If there aren't other FBA sellers with the product listed, it's a good bet you'll have no trouble selling it at a higher price since you'll have the benefits of Amazon's shipping policies, especially for Prime members. You can actually charge more than a manufacturer selling on Amazon since their Prime members are often willing to pay extra for quickly receiving the item. Additionally, that coveted "Buy Box" is going to be much easier to obtain if there aren't other FBA sellers.

Pay attention to the sales ranking of the item. This figure is displayed on the product page, and it gives a clear idea of how often the item sells compared to everything else on Amazon or within the category the ranking is for. Unless you have a rare item that isn't often available for sale, which is likely better sold elsewhere anyway, then it is best to stick to products with a ranking above 100,000 when possible. Items below this may simply sit around in the Amazon warehouses for ages and be a total waste of time and energy. If they sit there too long, you'll be forced to start paying long-term storage fees, and those can eat away at your profits fast.

There are plenty of places to source the products you will ultimately sell in your Amazon store, and thinking outside the box will often give you excellent results. Some common resources include:

Your Stuff

Using the scanning tool of the Amazon Seller app, make the rounds throughout your home, scanning items you may (or may not) want to sell. Anything with a barcode can simply be scanned. This is a great first step for your FBA business because it doesn't add to the startup costs, it helps to declutter your home a bit, and it helps you learn the process.

Good items to scan include:

- DVDs
- CDs
- Records
- Books
- Anything in packaging
- Anything with a barcode

You may also find some items without a barcode that are worth the effort of selling, but you'll have to manually search for these items on Amazon to determine the value and if it seems worth the costs and time involved. In general, finding barcodes makes life a lot easier.

You may be surprised how much stuff you have to sell that's just been sitting around. You will very likely be able to fill your first box with stuff you have sitting around the house. Make sure to check with your husband or wife before selling their stuff, though! This method is obviously not sustainable, but as a beginner, it's really what you should be doing. Let's move on to other options that are more sustainable.

Clearance Sections

Anytime you're at a retail store for any reason, take a few minutes to run through the clearance aisles and see if there is anything worth buying to resell. You may be surprised how often you find a decent item or two. Having the Amazon Seller app at the ready makes this a lot easier, as typing in each item's barcode while you're in the store can be a pain. It may seem a little weird walking around a store with a phone and scanning items, but don't let yourself feel uncomfortable. Everyone else is looking at their phones too, and they probably won't even notice you.

Items that are already listed on Amazon will be the easiest to grab and sell since it won't require you to create a new product page. Keep in mind that only professional seller accounts allow for new product page creation as well. We'll discuss in a moment how clearance aisles work within the concept of retail arbitrage.

Thrift Stores

There are plenty of items you can find at thrift stores, from books, CDs, DVDs, and records, to everything under the sun. The great thing about many thrift stores, especially chains like Salvation Army and Goodwill, is that they are constantly restocking their shelves, meaning you can literally go into them almost every day and find something new. Even with less popular thrift stores, they will likely be restocking fairly often. Go into these places and ask when they restock, when they have sales, etc. Many thrift stores provide a calendar for sales dates, so be sure to grab one if it is available.

When items like CDs and DVDs are new and unwrapped, these can be a great item to snag. Bring along the trusty Amazon Seller app to scan products and evaluate if they are viable options for selling through FBA. Used items can still be good, too, but new items tend to cause the least problems with returns and refund requestse. Media items are great to sell because the shipping costs involved in having a large amount of them sent to an Amazon fulfillment center is fairly lower than heavier, larger items. Again, don't let that stop you from scanning used items with a barcode, or if your knowledge about used and vintage items is good enough, feel free to research products that may not have a barcode as well, just keep in mind that the time involvement is increased.

The great thing about thrift stores is that some items will bring in far more than you're going to pay, and they're great learning spaces. With items like books and DVDs, you'll begin to notice certain patterns. Some items are far too common and not worth selling, and as you scan (with your eyes) through a bookshelf or DVD rack, you won't really need to scan (with your Amazon Seller app) to know that some items are just too common and aren't going to sell. Likewise, with books, you'll start to notice that text books and other nonfiction books tend to sell better than trade paperback fiction books. However, if you manage to get your hands on certain fiction novels, especially if they're new releases, first edition, or rare printings, they can be worth your while.

Yard Sales

Yard sales are like thrift stores, except the prices are often better and there's only one or two days in which you can claim the items appropriate for selling online. Much like thrift stores, searching for items in their retail packaging and media like CDs and DVDs is an easy place to start.

To get the most out of yard sales, it's best to have a plan of action. Map out the yard sales going on around you and try to hit the ones that seem like the best fit first thing in the morning. Other people are out there looking for great deals, and you may even be competing with other resellers, so an early start can be the difference between a great day and an okay day. Just be respectful when people ask that no early birds show up, or you may find yourself arguing with someone instead of finding a great deal.

All of the perks of thrift stores apply to yard sales too, but the limited availability and non-static nature of pop-up sales means that you have one shot. These can be a lot of fun and a great source of income, though, so don't write them off just because the location isn't going to offer repeat opportunities in the future.

As an added tip, if you know what kind of items you want to sell, you can always ask the sellers if they have anything else inside the house like those items and if they would be willing to let them go.

Craigslist and Facebook Buy/Sell/Trade Groups

Much like yard sales, the best way to score with Craigslist or Facebook sales group listings is to be one of the first responders. The quicker you get in, the more likely to receive the item you'll be. This takes patience, and some days will go much better than others. If you live in a remote area, these methods may not be the most fruitful, but if you live near a large city, your local pages are likely teeming with items ripe for the picking. On the other hand, there are probably a lot more resellers around too.

Auctions

Auctions can be hit or miss. Some auctions are going to have too many bidders, and the prices will extend beyond the three times rule quickly. Others may be cheap but not provide as much to choose from, and often they'll focus on antiques, furniture, and larger items that aren't worth selling through the FBA program. This isn't always the case, though.

On the other hand, there are storage locker and other types of mostly-blind auctions where you will only get a glimpse at everything you're bidding on. With these, a large amount of potential products can be bought for a low price. Not all of these items are going to be ideal for sales through Fulfillment by Amazon, but if your hustling includes selling locally as well, it may be worthwhile. Likewise, if the price is low enough, you can take what you want to sell and always simply donate the rest to thrift stores as a tax write off.

Online and Retail Arbitrage

Online arbitrage is finding retail items online, buying them, and then reselling them. This can be done through wholesalers, retail websites, eBay, and even Amazon sometimes. While finding brand new products online that meet the criteria of being able to sell for three times the amount they are purchased for may not always be easy, once you find some good resources, there's a fairly decent shot that they will continue to produce.

Going the route of wholesale is great, but the investment can be a bit daunting. Likely, you'll be purchasing large lots of a single product, so it needs to be an item that sells well. Nobody wants to sit on a pile of iPhone 4 cell phone cases while the iPhone 8 is about to be released. This is just bad for business and ultimately you'll lose money. For most, it is better to hold off on wholesale deals until the capital produced otherwise warrants it and your skills in determining products worth selling have improved.

Retail arbitrage involves getting off of your couch sometimes, but it can be a great source of income and new products to sell. We've basically already talked about this, but it can be expanded upon quite a bit. The obvious places to start are Walmarts, CVS', Targets, etc. The obvious places have the benefit of online shopping, ordering, and local pickup rather than walking around stores all day and scanning items. However, a mom and pop store can be a great source of items as well, and always exploring new potential options is key to success with this method. Closeout stores, outlets, and other off-the-beaten path options should never be overlooked.

To give you a better idea of how retail arbitrage works, let's look at an example. Browsing the Walmart clearance aisle, I've picked up an item that is listed as "LEGO BATMAN MOVIE The Batmobile 70905 Building Kit (581 Piece)" on Amazon. When I use the Amazon Seller app to scan the item and get some information on it, I can see that it's a popular selling item in the Toys category. Awesome, I should have no problem moving it. The going price is around $42.00 shipped with other Fulfillment by Amazon sellers, and since I paid around $15 for it, it comes very close to being able to sell for three times the amount. Not bad. There were two of them, so I grabbed them both.

The proceeds from my sale will be $42.00.

The referral fee charged is going to be $6.30 (15% of $42).

Taking away the cost ($15) and the referral fee leaves a profit of $20.70.

This is a return of 97.18%, with a profit margin of 49.29%.

Of course I bought both of them that were available, so I make this amount twice! Keep in mind that along the way, you will have also spent money to ship an entire box to Amazon, storage fees, etc. However, this gives you an idea of why retail arbitrage works so well. You literally can find these types of items online and pick them up or while walking through a store and handling other shopping needs. In ideal situations, you may be able to pick up more than just a couple of the same item. As you continue to work your way through stores and this process, it starts to become easier to notice which products are worth scanning and which are not.

Because these are likely to be brand name products, there is very little required in the way of marketing or content creation, making it easier for those that prefer not to become writers, photographers, and brand creators. However, it is totally possible to find yourself in a dry spell at times when using local resources, which makes for less-than-predictable income at times.

Private Label Products

Private label products are an excellent source of income when done correctly. In theory, the process is simple, but the execution is not for the lazy or those scared of risks. Rather than purchasing brand name items from a store (retail arbitrage), auctions, or other resources to resell through Amazon Seller Central, you create a product without actually putting in the research and development involved in creating the product. Instead, you find a product already available via wholesalers that are willing to put your brand name on the items and packaging, and you build a brand around these products.

There are many cons to this method, especially for a beginner. The most obvious con is the high cost of purchasing products in bulk and taking the risk that they may not sell. Unlike popular brand name items, people are not actively searching out the particular product name that you have. Instead, it becomes your job to market this product better than several of your competitors. It adds a whole new layer to your Amazon FBA-based business, and while many people might shy away from the content creation, logo designing, and constant marketing involved, the opportunity for significantly higher profits is there. This isn't a quick method for earning some money, but it is scalable in the best ways.

Don't let the cons completely deter you, though. It may not be the best method starting out, but as your business begins growing and you have better funds and understanding of the different markets and trends involved, private label branding and selling has many benefits. Not only is the product typically going to have a cheap cost per unit, but once a few items with your brand are well-reviewed and sell, it becomes easier to introduce new products in similar categories. Additionally, it takes the guess work out of trying to find products to sell, freeing up time for those other tasks involved in private label selling. Having this consistent resource for products is a god send for serial entrepreneurs that want to branch off into other areas as well. Spending all your time shopping isn't for everyone.

Because this method is a little more involved than others, I'll walk you through it step by step.

Step 1. Research Products

The first step is to consider what products you will brand. The good news is that there are methods to help determine if a product is going to be viable. Consider the following:

1. **Is there a national brand product that almost completely controls the market?** As a prime example, trying to sell unknown branded tablet computers is probably never going to work. Between Kindle (with budget tablets) and Apple (with high-quality and high-performance tablets), the tablet market doesn't leave a lot of elbow room for new brands. Likewise, something like DSLR cameras aren't viable because of huge brand names like Nikon. This doesn't mean it's impossible, but digging deeper into less dominated markets is ideal.

2. **Consider the sales rank on Amazon for the most popular products comparable to the product you want to distribute.** If the top three items are below 10,000, that means that demand is high. Otherwise, sales may be slow.

3. **How many reviews do those top three products have?** As a rule of thumb, it's difficult to compete with products that have 300+ reviews. It's not impossible, but it's going to take some serious marketing skills (and probably money).

4. **What can you sell the item for?** With private label, as with any venture where you're marketing a product, it's important to remember that every product is going to require large commitments in terms of marketing costs and time. As such, if a product cannot sell for more than $25, it is probably not going to be worth your time unless you're selling in huge amounts daily. While you may not want to sell very expensive products (less sales in general), you don't want to sell items that aren't going to bring a return on investment if they aren't sold in high volume.

5. **Who is your competition?** Especially in regards to other private label sellers, just how well are they actually doing their job? If you scout out some of the other sellers and see that their product listing copy is shoddy, their customer feedback scores are low, or other signs of doing a less-than-ideal job, then that means someone with the right gusto, skills, and motivation can surpass their products by creating a better brand (even if it's essentially the same item). Take time to read the reviews as well, and if there's something that sticks out as negative about the product that you believe you can remedy (such as: poor instructions or not including a small screwdriver to open the item for batteries), then that may be a golden opportunity to provide added value.

6. **How available is this type of product?** Can you easily buy it at Walmart or Target? It is probably not worth your time to sell a product traditionally purchased while grocery shopping or at very popular big box stores. While they may have similar items, yours should be less of a commodity.

7. **How much does it weigh?** Lighter items mean cheaper shipping costs, less packaging, lower handling fees from Amazon. Don't waste time on large products unless you're feeling extremely confident in your abilities.

8. **Is the product going to ship well?** As a private label seller, you're likely going to be purchasing products from China, then shipping them to Amazon, and then Amazon will ship them to the buyer. So, it goes to reason that any products you bother with private label branding needs to be something that's durable. Steer clear of anything glass!

9. **Could one person potentially buy the same product again?** The main reason for this would be that it's a great gift item or somehow consumable. While it is not a make or break consideration, it does help to consider if the same product would sell to the same person more than once.

10. **How many do you have to order at once?** Before even branding a product, does the wholesale provider allow you to buy a few at a time just to evaluate them? Not taking the time to check out a product before branding it is a HUGE

mistake, so when a wholesaler refuses to send a small order, you may need to find another source. At the same time, just how many do you need to purchase once you're ready to commit to the product? Is it going to be financially viable for your business and home to fund a huge order?

While it may be impossible to meet all of these criteria, getting as close as possible will help to alleviate the guesswork and amp up the likelihood of success! It's imperative that you spend time researching the products that will sell and ensuring the quality is up to par.

Step 2. Finding a Supplier

The most obvious source for a decent supplier is going to be sites like http://alibaba.com. These sellers are going to be in Asian countries, often China, and as such, shipping time will not always be quick. (Surprisingly, shipping is usually priced pretty fairly, though.) While you might source products in the United States, the cost effectiveness of that approach is likely to drown you in debt before you can even make a profit. Because you want to be able to mark up the product as much as three times the cost you're originally paying for it, Chinese-made goods are often your best bet.

You may be groaning at that thought, but just because it's made in China doesn't mean it's worthless. Search for your product and pull up a handful of suppliers for it. Research the supplier as much as possible to make sure they're trustworthy. Alibaba is extremely safe to use, but not all sellers are going to give you great service and products.

Once you've narrowed it down to a few potential suppliers, talk to them about branding the items. Many suppliers will gladly offer these services for packaging and item branding, and it can be a huge money-saving and time-saving benefit from working with Alibaba sellers.

Do not be afraid to negotiate. They want your business, and they may be willing to cut a deal. Remember that you want to TRY the item before buying it in bulk, so finding a supplier willing to sell you a few of them is going to go a long way. Not only does it mean you can test the items (you want to test more than one to check for consistency), but it also means that they are going to be flexible and easy to work with.

Step 3. Creating Brand Logos

If the product you purchased checks out, and you believe it is going to work well for your private label goals, then it's time to consider branding. Ideally, you'll have worked on this prior to receiving the first shipment of the product you've tested.

So before placing a large order with your branding on it, you'll need to have a logo and packaging design completed. Unless you're an excellent graphic designer already, you'll probably want to hire some help from a freelance designer on Upwork.com or Fiverr.com

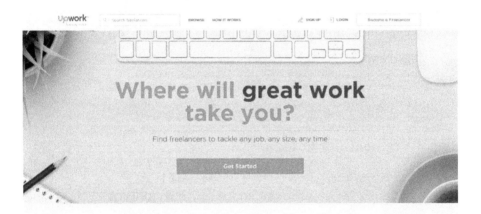

Work with someone perfect for your team

With Upwork, you'll be able to post a job and have people bid on it, giving you access to their profiles and often a portfolio of their previous work. Fiverr is a cheaper option, but just remember that you're likely going to be buying hundreds of the same product with the same logo, so it really needs to shine, and "you get what you pay for" is often the case with freelance work.

I'm going to sound mean for a second, but please do not hire your niece or nephew just because they're art students. A huge mistake many entrepreneurs make is working with friends and family that aren't quite ready for this level of design. If they are, that's amazing, but don't let personal connections cloud your judgment when you'll be spending large sums of money. Your business counts on you to make logical decisions.

Once the product design and logo are prepared, send them off to the supplier, and they'll begin the process of branding the item for you.

Step 4. Create Killer Content

It's disgustingly repeated over and over, but content is truly king when it comes to sales. Taking the time to produce high-quality, engaging sales copy is going to have a LOT to do with the success of a private label product designed to be sold through Amazon.

Because your supplier is both branding your product and shipping it from overseas, you may have at least a week or as long as a month to start working on your listing content. Take advantage of this time and try to produce some immaculate sales copy that's eye-catching, comprehensive, and clean. Include high quality images, describe the functions of the product, and make sure to point out why it's better than other similar products without specifically saying, "It's better than the Waddayacallit D3200!" If you're unfamiliar with the HTML that Amazon allows for listing, then hire someone to help you dress the listing content up after it is finished or take time to learn this coding (it's fairly limited, so it doesn't require a lot of effort to learn).

We mentioned this before, but a TON of sellers are doing a horrible job at this pivotal stage of private label selling. They're creating rushed, unedited content with no call to action, not enough details, and poor images. Even if a half-hearted job is enough to be better than your most obvious competitors, you need to absolutely SLAY this if you want to see sales that are worth all the time and effort you put into this product. This is not the place to skimp.

Step 5. List it on Amazon

Now that you've produce a great brand with a reliable product, received the shipment, and completely dominated the competition with solid listing content, it's finally time to actually list the product and send them off to Amazon for fulfillment. We'll discuss this process in detail in another chapter.

You'll likely put in additional time and money for marketing, but unlike retail or online arbitrage where you need to constantly source new items, your time should free up to begin working on your next private label product while this one generates you some passive income in the meantime.

Private label isn't the easiest method or choice, but when things start rolling, the passive income and safety of having an easy-to-source product becomes a huge benefit to your FBA-based business.

Learn the Selling Process First

Just because it seems like a good deal, that doesn't mean it is worth your time. Consider weight, popularity of the product, and the actual amount of profit you are likely to make. Always be asking yourself if the item is worth your time, money, and energy. Do not try to stock every single thing you come across, or you'll find yourself wasting a lot of hard work on nothing.

Always keep your eyes open. Once you get in the habit of looking for profits in items wherever you go, it will become easier to spot things that are profitable, and you will begin learning about the many categories and markets available through Amazon. Keeping your eyes open and an ear to the ground are keys to your success.

To help yourself understand the ins and outs of listing and selling products, if they are truly worth the time, and if they are going to be profitable, it's really best to start out by selling your own stuff. Not only is the financial investment much smaller, but it can give you an idea of what items you may want to keep an eye out for in the future.

Once you have a nice pile of items to sell, it is time to finally begin the process of listing, shipping to Amazon for fulfillment, and then starting the process over while finally raking in some earnings. However, before we jump into that, let's take a moment to consider how fees work.

Chapter 4: Understanding Seller Central and FBA Fees

To help with the sourcing of items and the listing process, it's a good idea to glean some understanding of the way the fee structures involved work. We mentioned that rule of three (where you should only buy a product if it can be sold for three times the cost), and these fees have a lot to do with that requirement.

While our main focus is selling with Fulfillment by Amazon, understanding the fees for sales that you fulfil yourself will help to understand the additional fees involved with Amazon fulfillment as well. Let's begin there.

Fulfilling Orders Yourself

When packaging and shipping an item to a buyer yourself, there are two major fees involved. First, there is the "referral fee." In most categories, the referral fee is going to be a static 15% of the total sale. However, this fee is sometimes lower for certain categories, such as home computer and photography gear.

The other fee involved is the "variable closing cost" fee. This fee is $1.35 for any media, such as books, video games, or music items. For other items, the fee is generally only $0.45 cents plus $0.05 cents per pound in weight.

These fees are based on the sales price, and it does not include any shipping costs. As an example, consider what happens when you sell a textbook sold for $25.

$25 for the item

+ $3.99 shipping credit

- $3.75 "15% referral fee"

- $1.35 "variable closing cost"

= $23.89 deposited into your Amazon Seller Central Account.

When selling without Fulfillment by Amazon, any shipping labels purchased from Amazon will be taken directly out of your current balance. Should the shipping be less than the shipping credit, you get to keep the change. Should the shipping be higher, then you have to eat those additional costs. Keep in mind that you will also be paying for any shipping materials used, ink for your printer, printer paper or sticker labels, etc.

Fees While Using Fulfillment by Amazon

Moving forward, let's consider how fees work with Fulfillment by Amazon. I explain the fees without just so you can compare.

Much like the standard method of packaging and fulfilling your orders yourself, the referral fee still applies despite using Amazon's fulfillment services. However, the shipping credits you would receive are no longer applicable. For small, cheaply priced, cheap-to-ship items, that may mean less revenue.

Keep in mind that FBA isn't a free service either. On top of the usual referral fee, the fee structures involved with FBA depend largely on your choices and the items you happen to stock.

With the "Individual" plan (free), fees include pick and pack, weight handling, and storage.

Storage fees fluctuate throughout the year, and for this reason, it's wise to consider what you're willing to keep stored in the warehouses and for how long. Additionally, larger items may be considered "oversized" and incur an increased storage fee.

The "pick and pack fee" is that $0.99 cent cost per item we spoke of earlier. Again, if you're selling more than 40 items per month, it's time to upgrade to the professional Seller Central account, as these fees are completely removed with the professional account. This is the only fee that changes with the professional account over the individual account, but a dollar per sale can be a huge difference.

Because these fees are sometimes updated, it is better to get an idea of the costs by visiting the Amazon page that covers them. You can find those at http://goo.gl/5u9bSd.

While it's true that the fees involved with FBA takes away additional cost, a high-volume seller is going to make up the difference by having more time to work on sourcing new products. In most cases, the benefits of having Amazon fulfil your orders is such a time saver that you will ultimately save money as well (even if it doesn't seem that way when you look at your Amazon reports).

The Quick Solution

By now, you're probably groaning at the idea of calculating all of these fees and trying to determine if an item is even worth selling, especially if you made the mistake of purchasing it for more than one-third the amount you can sell it at. The good news is that SaleCalc exists. SaleCalc is a simple website that allows you to type in your product cost, desired selling point, and a host of other details that determine roughly what the fees and profits for each item will be.

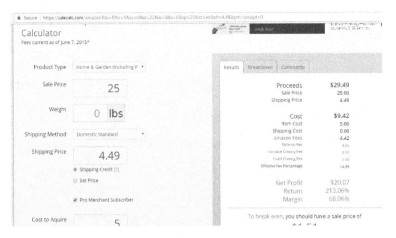

SaleCalc.com

Make sure to bookmark the website http://salecalc.com. This website will save you a ton of time. They do a solid job of keeping everything updated, but be sure to check that it has been updated recently or the information you receive may be slightly off. They also provide fee services for a number of other online marketplaces should you need them.

Amazon Revenue Calculator

Recently, Amazon also rolled out a revenues calculator, and it is more powerful and more useful than SaleCalc when your only source of sales is Amazon. Take a look at it by navigating to https://sellercentral.amazon.com/hz/fba/profitabilitycalculator/index?lang=en US, and you'll quickly see how useful it can be.

Almost There…

Understanding the fees helps to justify the low cost you must procure items for, but it also enables you to understand which items are going to be worthwhile for selling. Take the time to learn the costs involved with storage for the current season, and determine if keeping all of your items in the warehouse for seasons where they're less likely to sell is worth it.

Now that you understand where to find items and how to get a rough idea of the fees involved, it's time to consider the listing process.

Chapter 5: Listing Products on Amazon Seller Central

Now that you have a nice little collection of items to sell, it's time to begin listing products for sale and getting them prepped for shipment to Amazon's warehouses, also known as fulfillment centers. It is ideal to handle these listings on a computer rather than trying to handle them all on a smartphone. Not only are you going to need to print stuff later (much easier on a PC/MAC than a smartphone), but the entire process is just a lot easier this way.

Step 1. Evaluate Products and Pricing

Log into your Amazon Seller Central account, and on the menu, find where it says "Inventory." Place your cursor over this, and from the menu options displayed, select "Add a Product."

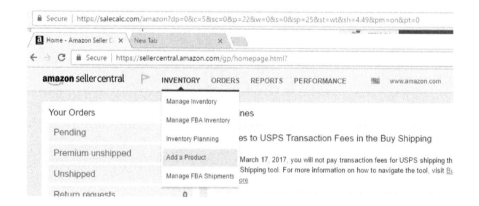

This will bring us to a page asking to identify the items. If the item has a barcode, there are two options. Either type in the barcode or use the scanner (optional gear mentioned earlier) and simply scan the barcode. The scanner will really save a lot of time and help avoid errors in typing out the numbers.

Most of the time, the item is probably already available on Amazon for sale. Make sure it is the correct item, size, color, and every other detail. Most of the time this won't be a huge concern, but when it is, listing an item incorrectly usually means returns and/or refunds. Click on the product to see the details.

Under the description, there will be offers for the products. This includes both new and used offers; click whichever one best represents the item being listed. Do not list used items as new.

The following page will show the prices that other sellers are offering the product for, and on this page are also short descriptions of the products and their condition. When selling through Fulfillment by Amazon, the major competition is other Fulfillment by Amazon sellers. While other sellers may be competition still, they receive none of the perks of being shipped and handled by Amazon, and often people will purchase a FBA item over a random seller item, especially Prime members enjoying the quick and free shipping.

Taking a look at other FBA sellers and their prices for the product, we can learn how best to price the item. In most scenarios, if the product is of the same quality, it is best to at least match the lowest price available. This helps sales in two ways. First, the item appears near the top of the list in relation to other FBA sellers. Second, the "Buy Box" on product pages are almost always from FBA sellers, and this increases the chances of becoming the seller whose item is sold when someone doesn't evaluate offers and takes the quickest route of purchase. Keep in mind that a professional seller account is required for this perk.

To make this process a bit easier, certain search options are available. With these search restrictions, it is possible to view only the Prime and free shipping items, which weeds out all the extra sellers who aren't direct competition. There will be a clear marking next to a seller's name that says, "Fulfillment by Amazon."

That said, sometimes a product is worth listing a bit higher to make the profit required from it. If it can be listed confidently at a higher price and the seller is patient, this can ultimately bring in better profits and return on investment. On the flip side, avoid underselling other FBA sellers. Anytime people start to price items lower and lower, a price war is likely to ensue, which translates to everyone losing money. Don't fall into that trap. Price MATCH, don't try to undercut!

Going back to the Seller Central page, which should have remained open in a separate tab or window, there will be a "Sell Yours" link next to the product. Click on this to begin listing the product on the following page. The following steps will cover the required fields on this page.

Step 2. Condition Notes

The condition notes are about the only content that most sellers ever create. Even if you're not a great writer, this should be taken seriously. Far too many sellers simply copy and paste the same condition notes for everything. While that may save time, it can also lead to lower sales and more returns/refunds. Writing honest and complete descriptions for each item helps your business stand out amongst the competition.

With any opened media items, test them and include a note that they are tested and working. For new items, mention that they are brand new in packaging. You can reiterate obvious facts like the free two-day shipping offered by Amazon, and explain the methods used to ensure the item remains in great condition.

Do NOT skimp on these condition notes. For those buyers that don't simply click the "Buy" button, these notes, the prices, and the feedback score you have are usually large parts of the decision to purchase from one seller over another, especially since prices are likely to be close to one another.

Step 3. Pricing and Shipping Options

At this stage, you should have already determined the best way to price the item. If you haven't, return to Step 1. Add in the price.

Scroll down to the bottom of the page, and in the shipping options, select the one that says, "I want Amazon to provide customer service for my items if they sell." This is how you begin the FBA process. Click "Save and Continue."

Step 4. Create a Shipping Plan

Since you have chosen to have Amazon handle customer service, the next page contains a prompt to create a new shipping plan. Choose "individual products" for the packing type. The follow page will list the product and ask you to enter the quantity of the product you intend to ship to an Amazon fulfillment center. Click on "Save."

Now, it's time to repeat the above steps until all the items you wish to send to Amazon are listed. While doing so, make sure to place all of the products within the same shipping plan (the one you just created) rather than creating a new one for each. The more products to ship at the same time, the better, as this will keep shipping costs down.

When the list is finally complete, click "Continue" on the screen that lists your products allocated within the shipping plan.

Step 5. Information on Prepping Items

The next page will ask for your address. Simply enter this and continue.

Following this, Amazon will provide a list of requirements for how items are prepped and packaged. Common requirements include packaging items in poly bags, putting items in their own boxes, or bubble wrapping items for extra protection. Not following these requirements can cause problems, so never skip this step. It is advised to make notes on this or screen shot the page to review later, as we typically handle this step later in the process.

The item is ready to be listed, but it won't be listed until after Amazon receives it. The next steps are getting everything labeled, packaged, and shipped to Amazon for fulfillment. We'll cover this in the next chapter since it's so involved.

Chapter 6. Packing and Setting Up Shipments to Amazon

Now that you've listed your items and had them setup for sale through Fulfillment by Amazon, it's time to prepare your boxes to ship. Do not skimp or skip anything during this process, as your success depends on your ability to follow Amazon's requirements to ensure everything goes smoothly.

Step 1. Clean Everything

If you're selling any used goods or new goods with dust on the boxes, you'll unfortunately have to take the time to clean them up prior to packaging and shipping them. This part can seem like a time waster, but sending dirty products to customers is an easy way to get poor reviews and lose future business.

Start by removing any price tags. You do not want them to know that you paid a fraction of the cost they paid. To remove any of the sticky residue, you can use products like Goo Gone or just a little rubbing alcohol if it won't damage the packaging. Be careful while removing labels and cleaning, as any imperfects will make the item appear used even if it isn't.

Step 2. Prepping Your Items

If the item is in retail packaging that's undamaged, you can easily leave it as is. If it isn't, you will need to box or bag your product before placing any barcode labels on them. It is recommended that you bubble wrap items before bagging them. Boxing items when it's unnecessary should be avoided, as the costs are much too high for little in return.

Step 3. Labeling Items

Labeling is the next important step. Per the earlier recommendation, Avery 5160 (30) size labels are perfect for this application.

To print your labels, return to your product inventory by logging in at Seller Central, and clicking "Products Amazon Fulfills" under the "Inventory" tab. This will bring you to a page with all of your products awaiting labels and shipping. From here, check the items you are going to ship, and then from the drop down menu above or below, choose "Print Item Labels."

The following page will show you the items, and at the bottom is a drop down menu that lets you choose the printing method and label sizes. If you've chosen to use the Avery 5160 (30) sized labels, it should automatically be chosen as the default. Once you're prepared, click "Print Item Labels."

Here, Amazon will remind you that you'll be placing these barcode labels over the existing barcodes. If the barcode area is too small for your label, you can cover it with a white label and place the barcode elsewhere, but you MUST cover the existing barcode.

The result is a PDF that's downloadable, which you can then print. The barcodes should be easy to manage since they include the name of the item on them in most situations. If the item is cleaned and ready, place this barcode over the original barcode, follow the notes you took earlier concerning Amazon's requirements for packaging (remember, some items must be bagged or boxed per their requirements), and place it in the correct box for shipping. Repeat this with all of your products until you're ready to ship.

Note that you can setup labeling by Amazon instead. This costs $0.20 per label, so it's a huge waste of your money since labeling really doesn't take very long at all. Only do this if you're selling massive quantities and really don't have the time or can't hire someone to help out.

Step 4. Shipping Your Box

Now that you've labeled all your items, fulfilled Amazon's requirements for packaging, and placed the items in the box securely, it's time to finally ship to Amazon for their fulfillment services. You've made it. This is almost time to celebrate a little!

Returning to your FBA inventory, you should be able to select all the items you've already labeled, and then from the drop down menu, choose "Send/Replenish Inventory."

Since we've already labeled and prepped our items, we can click "Review Shipments" on the follow page. This should tell you the places each item needs to go along with the name of the shipment. Note that you won't always be sending all products to the same distribution warehouse, so it's important not to package up your boxes before this step.

If you have more than a single shipment package on this page, you can click the "View contents" link beside each of the shipments to be made to see which products should go in which box. Package up your boxes as you go. Do not seal your boxes yet.

If everything is in the box where it belongs, choose "Approve Shipments," and you'll be able to purchase shipping for your packages. To finish this step, you'll have to weigh and measure your boxes, input this data into the shipping page, and select the appropriate carrier for the job. Most of the time, UPS is the route to go. Click "calculate" and Amazon will give you pricing and the option to print out your shipping labels.

You can simply tape your labels onto your boxes, but if you prefer adhesive printer paper, the best size for these box labels is Avery 8465, which has an adhesive label on each side of a standard sized sheet of printer paper. Once printed, remove both of the labels and place them on the box in a way that they cannot be sliced down the middle while it's being opened by Amazon's warehouse staff. Generally, the two top halves of the box are perfect. Take it to the UPS drop off, do a little celebratory dance, and start working on finding new products to continue growing your business. Amazon will let you know once your products have arrived and are ready for sale!

Chapter 7. Reading Your Reports

Once you've sent off a package, it's time to start sourcing more goods for your Amazon Seller Central ambitions, but it's also time to learn the ins and outs of what Amazon can offer in terms of reporting. The reports page can be found in the top navigation menu. Clicking on "Reports" will likely bring you to an overview of the section, but we'll describe it here in less convoluted detail so you can manage reporting with ease.

Inventory Reports

Inventory reports are designed to help you understand the inventory you have in stock, what is currently unavailable for sale, and a host of other situations. These reports are a quick way to export your inventory to Excel or other spreadsheet programs. There are a lot of different reports available, so we'll cover a handful of the more useful ones.

1. **Inventory Age** – The inventory age report helps you keep tabs on just how long some of your items have been sitting in warehouse limbo. This report is ideal for determining if it's time to pull some products from the warehouse and stop wasting money on the storage fees. Because Amazon charges additional fees for long-time storage, browsing this report every month or so is vital to avoiding unnecessary costs. In addition, it will give you some idea of ways to help move aged inventory, such as showing you the lowest price, your list price, and details about how many you have sold in the past.

2. **Bulk Stranded Inventory** – "Stranded" inventory is inventory that is stored in the warehouses yet unavailable for sale for one reason or another. This report is generally for items sold in bulk, and the information it provides is a useful tool to help solve common problems that may result in items not being for sale, such as incomplete listings, no product listing available, or not marked as being fulfilled by Amazon. This great tool is only available if you are currently a professional seller on Amazon.

3. **Stranded Inventory** – Similar to the bulk report, except it focuses on individual products and does not require a professional seller account (but you should really have one). It is worth noting that while these stranded inventory reports

are useful, you should be receiving emails from Amazon when items aren't making it onto the site for sale, so if you're proactive, these may not be that necessary, but if you aren't able to solve problems as they arise, handling them is easier with these reports.

4. **Reserved Inventory** – Reserved items are typically items that are in the process of being purchased (waiting on a credit card to clear) or in the process of shipment. The real-time data provided here makes it easy to see the status of these items.

5. **Fulfilled by Amazon** – This report is only generated as a spreadsheet, and while it is near real-time, orders can be placed at any moment making the data less than reliable; however, it does help to assess the products currently in storage and awaiting sale.

6. **Inventory Health** – The inventory health provides details on a host of data from sales made to items available or unavailable for sale but still in storage. In addition, it helps to fully assess if items need to be adjusted to help incur more sales.

Take the time to explore your inventory reports after you've started selling for a month or two, and you will find out which reports help you the best.

Sales Reports

Sales reports are great for tracking the sales made. While there are other ways to check these figures, the reports are perfect for selecting a past month and getting a full reporting of the sales that have occurred.

1. **Fulfilled by Amazon Reports** – Accurate data exported as a TXT file.

2. **All Orders (XML)** – Exports your sales as a spreadsheet for accurate bookkeeping.

3. **Customer Shipment Sales** – Reporting with condensed information concerning time of sale, item information, and location of sales. The location can give you an idea of where products are selling, which can be helpful for marketing should you go the route of private label sales.

4. **Promotions** – This report covers any products sold with certain Amazon promotions, such as Super Saver Shipping. This helps to assess when these promotions are helping sales.

Payments (to Amazon)

Payments reports cover payments to Amazon. These reports give a clear financial picture to the costs involved with your business and can be key in making sure your books are correct and consider every possible detail. These include:

1. **Monthly Storage Fees** – An intuitive breakdown of all the storage fees associated with your FBA products. This reporting tool is new, and it packs a lot of extra power in understanding the costs involved with storage, as well as helping determine if long-time or oversized item storage fees are worthwhile for items that aren't selling well.

2. **Fee Preview** – Perhaps one of the most important reports available, the fee preview report provides data on the estimated costs involved in the sale and shipment of your Fulfillment by Amazon products. These fees are estimations based on Amazon's current fee structure, and they may not always be perfectly accurate.

3. **Long-term Storage Fees** – This report evaluates the long-term storage fees incurred by product, allowing you to determine the costs involved and if it is worthwhile to continue paying long-term storage fees. Because long-term storage doesn't start for a year, it's a safe bet that this report is an easy way to determine if products need to be pulled from the Fulfillment by Amazon program.

4. **Reimbursements** – Reimbursements happen when products are damaged by warehouse staff, received by customers broken, or are returned or refunded for any reason. This report helps you understand the causes of these reimbursements.

Customer Concession Reports

Customer Concession reports revolve around refunds, returns, and any replacements made. At their discretion, Amazon may issue a refund, allow a return, or send out a replacement item (if possible) when a customer has an issue. These reports evaluate those issues to help remedy the problems in the future whenever possible.

1. **FBA Customer Returns** – This provides data on all returns and refunds given to customers. The useful thing about this report is that it will let you know if items are unsellable after return, meaning that you need to take action to either have Amazon ship it back to you (for a fee) or have them destroy the item on your behalf (free). In some cases, a returned item can be shipped back to Amazon and sold as a used item instead of a new item.

2. **Replacements** – In the event that you have multiple of the same product and a customer receives one in a less-than-ideal condition, Amazon may issue a replacement for this product. This report lists the details of those replacements,

helping you analyze the costs involved and pinpoint why the replacement happened. In the even that you're selling a private label product and returns or replacements are frequent, this report may help assess the situation.

Removal Reports

Additional reports to help you avoid paying too much for long-term storage fees. The notable report in this category is the "Suggested Removal Report," which will give you detailed information on those products you have for sale that are coming near to the long-storage fee dates (generally 12 months). These reports also include information on items removed and should you choose to receive those items back from Amazon, information on the shipments involved. You can opt to have Amazon dispose of these items if it isn't worth the work to have them shipped back to you for sale elsewhere.

Payment Reports

Leaving the long list of reports available, you can also use the Reports under the Report drop down menu on the top navigation bar to see additional information. The most obvious place to start is your payments. By default, this will provide your current earnings (or balance due) and explain the next scheduled payment date. Payments are generally weekly.

Within these payment reports, you can also view it as a list of transactions. Keep in mind that these are the financial transactions and do not include any product information.

If you go to the "All Statements" link, you'll be given a list featuring all transaction periods. This information is good for a quick overview of earnings, but it is not a dedicated method for book keeping.

Lastly, there is the option of "Date Range Reports" that make it easy to generate customer reports with set date ranges to help you understand your earnings. These reports are downloaded as spreadsheet files, so you'll be required to have Excel or similar software.

Tax Document Library

Returning to the "Report" drop down menu by hovering over the word "Report," we can navigate to "Tax Document Library." Here you will find all of your tax documents. Typically, this is going to be 1099K forms, but this only applies if you have sold $20,000 and met 200 sales. It is worth noting that just because Amazon Seller Central does not provide you with a tax document, that doesn't mean that you shouldn't be reporting your earnings. Consult with your tax professional on the best way to move forward should you not meet those requirements. If you did meet those requirements, this is where you can easily access tax forms for future reference.

Study Your Reports

The reporting features are very robust with Amazon, and it will take some personal experience to understand just how much it can benefit you to review how your business is running. Taking advantage of these reporting tools is crucial to avoiding making the same mistakes more than once, such as leaving items in storage for too long and incurring additional charges from long-term storage fees, or trying to sell an item that is defective and has a lot of returns or refunds involved with it.

If you believe there are discrepancies with your accounts, the reporting features may very well be the best line of defense for determining if these are truly errors on Amazon's part or if there's something else going on behind the scenes. When you're not the one handling customer service and shipments, these reports are your eyes and ears and should not be taken for granted.

Chapter 8. Case Study – My First $1,000 (and Beyond) Through FBA

Up to this point, the information I've shared with you has been largely technical, but it is important to remember that this isn't a guaranteed process, and there are a multitude of variables involved. For the beginner, it can be a huge learning curve to reach a point where the potential starts to feel tangible. To help encourage you, I'd like to share the story of how I made my first $1,000 through Fulfillment by Amazon.

I began my journey in basically the same manner most people take when selling online. I'd had some minor success selling random stuff on eBay here and there, and I had started running into some of the same resellers at yard sales and thrift stores. As the retro video game craze started to really blow up, it was still easy to find some extremely cheap game carts that were in decent shape and probably twenty years old yet sold for high dollar amounts. One of the resellers who was surprisingly nice to me considering we were competing for the same resell items told me that he made more money on Amazon than eBay, and that for some reason people were willing to spend more money on Amazon.

Naturally, more money is a good thing, and if I can find people who will happily pay more for the same product, why wouldn't I try that route? Soon after, I started my Amazon Seller Central account, and I listed some video games, CDs, books, and a few other items up for sale. I probably only had fifteen products, all of which I'd intended on selling through eBay or Facebook pages.

In my naïve newbie state of mind, I instantly figured it was wise to price my items below the lowest priced item available. While this did garner sales of popular items quickly, it ultimately lost me money, because given the condition of my products, I could have easily sold them for a bit more than the lowest going prices. Still, I made a profit, and after figuring out the fees and costs, it did seem that I made slightly better off than eBay. However, those items that didn't sell were quickly pushed down the price list by sellers who had the same (not so) bright idea. Only a few items dipped much lower than the original price, but the few bidding wars made those items almost not worth selling, but I left them listed as-is for the time being.

I always took the time to take pictures of my products and write a nice description for the condition notes. This is a great way to encourage sales and customer feedback. They have a good idea of what they'll receive when they get it, and that means that returns usually only occurred if the customer was nitpicking. As a writer, it was only natural that my content was pretty solid. As a person who thrives on honesty, my descriptions included even the most minor of blemishes.

Those items I left listed as-is weren't quick selling items, but when they sold for more than the lowest listed price, I realized that I'd messed up before. A little bit of patience would have helped me increase my profits.

This continued for awhile unchanged. I would shop at thrift stores and yard sales mostly, and sell media, toys, and electronics with my free Amazon Seller Central account. When I ran into that same reseller again, he told me that Amazon FBA has made his life a lot easier, and since he loved "the hunt" of buying, it saved him a lot of hassle shipping. I'd heard about FBA by this point, but given my small number of items on occasion, using this seemed like overkill. That was until I bought six boxes of mostly new Nintendo games from a man who had owned a store. He gave me a killer deal, just trying to liquidate his leftovers.

In total, I probably had two hundred products that I now needed to list and sell. Not only did I need to list and sell them, but I would also have to package them, ship them, handle any customer complaints, and practically handle every step of the way. It was clear that it was time to upgrade to a professional account and look into FBA.

I made a lot of mistakes. I was eager and rushed through the process. During the labeling stage, I labeled almost an entire box of games incorrectly and had to painstakingly pull off the labels, use goo gone to clean them up, and then reprint and reapply these labels to each item. If I had only read the instructions or done a little bit of research that would never have happened! It's such a rookie mistake that I still think about it every time I'm getting prepared to list my items and work on my shipments.

I didn't bother researching my products at all. I just looked at prices and matched the lowest FBA price (I must have read about this somewhere, as this is the ideal way to handle pricing). If I had taken the time to consider the sales ranking on some of the games, I would have realized that it would never have been worth my time to even sell them via Amazon. There are products that almost simply never sell, and I had at least fifty of them that I listed. They sat in storage until Amazon warned me that I was nearing my long-term storage fee dates so many months later, so I told Amazon to just dispose of them for me. While it didn't mean that I lost money overall, it was still a huge waste of time, energy, and money regardless. I could have easily skipped listing them and sold them in a huge lot for a dollar a piece or so.

I made other mistakes, but I also had success in many ways. Pricing the games at a low cost while in the FBA program meant that buyers with Prime were able to get them shipped to their door in two days without any extra costs to them. Those games that normally sell, sold very quickly, racking up between $4-10 per sale after all fees involved. There were a few games that sold for much higher.

I hadn't remotely sold everything, but at the end of two months, I had earned roughly $500 after fees and shipping costs by selling roughly half of my entire inventory. This took two months, but keep in mind that during that entire period I had really only wiped them off, labeled them, packaged them in a box, and shipped them all in a few days. The rest of the two months I did little else besides buying several other games, movies, records, and electronics for the same purpose. I didn't spend any time getting them together for Amazon until I realized sales were simply stopping with my first huge batch of products. That was a mistake, but when I found myself with some downtime, I finally started the process over.

So not only did I have 100 product listings on Amazon, many of which would never sell, but I also had another 100 or so products just sitting in my closet. I had to wipe them down, remove any price tags and stickers, and prep them for shipping if I wanted to earn back the money I'd spent on all the junk!

I learned my lesson about pricing already, and given the large quantity of items left in my inventory that was barely selling, I knew I needed to be more selective about what went online for sale and what didn't. Unlike the giant box, most of the items I had now were handpicked, but in fear of wasting money on storage fees (keep in mind, I wasn't earning that much at the time), I went through with the Amazon Seller app and actually bothered to scan the items, get an idea of how well they sold, and only listed those items that seemed worthwhile. Out of roughly 100 or so items, I probably listed $3/4^{th}$ of them, all priced specifically at the lowest FBA price available unless the quality was far superior.

These curated picks were much more fruitful. Once Amazon received my order, it was almost literally the day after the listings were live that I woke up and checked my accounts to find that over $500 worth of products had already sold. A few were higher priced items, but many of them were relatively cheap movies and video games that were popular sellers.

Realistically, at this point, I was just about breaking even between all the fees and the original costs, but I had earned in two days what I previously earned in two months. A lot of this success was because of some of the items I picked up, but ultimately, I attribute it to writing great condition notes, taking pictures (when it made sense to), and listing the products at the same price as other FBA sellers. It doesn't hurt that it was around Christmas time.

Those results aren't that excited, though, are they? I didn't think you would be impressed, but I wanted to give you an idea of what it's like being a beginner that doesn't take the time to do their research.

Following this success, I was hell-bent on making Amazon FBA a method of quitting my day job. I took that $500 I'd just made, and I spent it on wholesale lot auctions on eBay, buying some of the same types of media items. There was a lot of risk involved since most of these were boxes of DVDs, books, or games, and there are many of those items that don't sell well, but my results were similar the second time around. Products started to sell consistently because I only bothered with products that were worth selling .I didn't waste any time on items that had sales ranks higher than 100,000, and the results were obvious. Keep in mind, I still had a large inventory of my first large shipment to Amazon just sitting there and wasting away, costing me money for storage.

Within another month, I'd earned a decent $500-600 again, with many products still listed for sale, and I took that money to reinvest in more products. By now, I was finally wise that research actually pays off. I had learned about retail arbitrage (I'd never even considered reselling items from Walmart), and I made my way around Facebook groups, Craigslist, Walmarts, Targets, drug stores, etc. Then came one of those hundred mile-long yard sales, and the prices were CHEAP! I literally took vacation time from work to scour through the sales, scanning and buying things along the way that I believed I could sell for at least three times the amount I paid.

This huge sale really tipped me over. I managed to get so many good deals on higher end items that sell easily that after Amazon processed the shipment and another month had passed, I'd earned over $2,000 after spending less than $500 total.

Did I have to get up and look hard for product? Yes. Did I make mistakes and lose money? Definitely! That's the beauty of being an entrepreneur sometimes, but after these successes, I really buckled down and started to learn the ropes from seasoned sellers. With help from a mentor figure, I was able to find a wholesale product and earn over $1,500 in actual profits, and the proceeds were easily five times the amount that I had paid for the product. I quit my job after this, and that was the messy beginning of my serial entrepreneurship. If someone that made as many dumb mistakes as I did can succeed, I'm sure you can too.

Chapter 9. Make Your First $1,000 on FBA

Following my story with getting my toes wet in FBA and making a huge amount of mistakes, it seems wise to give you a plan of action to make your first $1,000-2,000 on FBA. Hindsight is always 20/20, and this is how I wish I had started things off because it would have taught me all the lessons I learned the hard way.

Step 1. Gather Supplies, Sign Up, Upgrade to Professional Plan

We've went over all the items you'll need to get started, so begin there, and while you're waiting for items to ship or once you're ready to move forward, sign up for your seller account and download the Amazon Seller app. Upgrade to the professional plan on Seller Central. It will cost you $40, but for this plan to work, we really want to sell more than 40 items anyway.

Step 2. Clean Out Your Closets

For your first $1,000, at least part of this should simply be items around your house that you don't really need. This includes DVDs, CDs, records, video games, books, electronics, anything you got for Christmas but never used, etc. This should make up at least a roughly estimated $250 of your first $1,000. Use the Amazon Seller app to scan these items, and use the revenue calculator to estimate your earnings. If you can't make it to roughly $250, you'll need to overcompensate a bit on the next steps.

Go ahead and list these items for sale. If there are enough to bother with a shipment, ship them for fulfillment, and the earning will begin while you continue.

Step 3. Hit the Ground Running with Retail Arbitrage

While I think most successful FBA sellers eventually move away from going into every store and scanning anything that seems to be on sale, this really is the best way to start out. The risk/reward is lower than trying to jump headfirst into wholesale.

Where I live, this would mean going to the SPCA thrift shop, Goodwill, Walmart, Target, Lowes, Home Depot, Big Lots, Ross, TJ Maxx, Kohls, and many others. If there is a shopping center around, starting here is great since so many stores are located together and don't require a ton of gas or time simply traveling around. Outlet malls are even better.

Do not buy anything that cannot be sold at a price of three times the amount you've paid for it. You won't always have time to calculate actual profits while you're shopping, so this rule of thumb is your best bet to avoid losing any money on products that aren't worth selling.

This process could take a few days, but you should be able to calculate another opportunity for earnings of at least $250, if not significantly more.

Step 4. Facebook, Craigslist, Free Stuff

You should be shopping Craigslist pretty religiously. Not only can you sometimes find great deals, but you can also post ads for certain items that you believe will sell. Additionally, there are a lot of free listings on Craigslists, and while many of the items may not be worth a ton of money, they are free, so if they're viable to sell, the cost of shipping isn't really a huge concern. Try to take advantage of these while remembering that light items are better to sell than heavy items.

Unless you live in the middle of nowhere (and sometimes even if you do), you likely have a handful of Facebook groups that service people buying, selling, and trading in your area. Take advantage of these as well. Much like Craigslist, you can post ads for the types of things you'd like to buy and resell.

This method should easily be able to bring in an additional $250 worth of profit in products.

Step 5. Yard Sales and Flea Market

On the weekend, get up early and make your way to any yard sales and flea markets you can. The generally low prices at these sales are going to make for a lot of easy profit if you find anything decent. If you find a box or pile of items you might be able to sell, try to buy the entire thing for a deeply discounted rate.

For example, if someone has a nice selection of roughly 50 DVDs priced for $1 a piece, offer them $25 to take them all off their hands at once. This particular example works well at yard sales. The worst they can do is tell you, "No thanks," and if you're lucky they'll meet you somewhere in the middle.

If there are any multi-family yard sales or church rummage sales, you absolutely should be attending them. These tend to have lower prices and great amount of variety.

Again, you should fairly easily be able to net the remaining $250 worth of profit from products through this method. In fact, if you've done all four of these methods for sourcing products over a two-week period, I'd be surprised if you didn't end up with more than $1,000 worth of profits should everything sell.

Step 6. List and Ship to Amazon, Wait for Profits.

Anything that hasn't been listed and shipped to Amazon, go ahead and do that now. If you haven't reached an estimated worth of $1,000, just repeat the steps above throughout the next week, and you should be able to make up the difference.

Step 7. Take Notes

This is really the importance of the "your first $1,000" exercise. Your first $1,000 is just a small milestone in a long list of success stories you will have. What you learn from non-discriminately shopping pretty much every local resource available is that what seems to work for you may not be what works for others. Which of the items that caught your eye were actually extremely viable? Which ones sold immediately after the listing went live, and which sat around (or remain in storage still)? All of this is important because for your next $1,000, you will now know what to ask for when you post ads on Craigslist to buy stuff. You will also know what to stop and look at when you're browsing through a yard sale, which stores seem to produce well for you, and you're beginning to learn how to interact with people through social media in a laid back but semi-professional manner. Ultimately, you may have worked pretty hard for that first $1,000, especially in regards to time, but the information you learned along the way is the real payout.

Chapter 10. Scaling Your FBA Business

Some minor success should fuel the fire, but that means a lot of hard work is ahead if your FBA business is going to be more than a mild success. There is no get-rich-quick method. You may have a wildly successful month, but you are still going to have to work hard to make sure the next month is also wildly successful, at least until you're established. Here are some of the secrets to helping you work ON your business instead of working FOR your business.

Don't Burn Out on Retail Arbitrage

The major problem most entrepreneurs face when trying to scale up their Amazon FBA business is the deadly burnout that makes them not want to ever step foot in a store or list another item on Amazon again. This happens when we hit the ground running too hard and sell too many one-off products.

If you love shopping, you may never burn out on that particular process. If you don't mind typing up condition notes while you watch TV, then you are a true warrior. However, that only goes so far. There are only so many days in a week, so many hours in a day, and at some point you simply aren't going to be able to scale any further if everything you sell is sold in quantities of one. If you keep trying to go this route, you almost inevitably burn out without seeing a huge increase in profits. Even if you don't quit, that's called "maintaining," and that's probably not your goal.

At this stage, you're almost your own employee instead of being your own boss. There are a ton of perks to retail arbitrage, but it isn't the end-all be-all for everyone making a living on Amazon FBA. Of course, some people stick to this method and do well.

Move Into Wholesale

One of the huge perks of starting off with retail arbitrage is that you have the opportunity to learn about a lot of different categories and products. If you take the time to review your sales and understand what seems to sell easily and what doesn't, what is easy to find cheap but sells high, then it goes to reason that you can take that knowledge and extend it into wholesale.

The perks of wholesale are plentiful. Not only are you getting the best possible deal for the products you're going to sell, but you also eliminate the constant pricing and scanning of new products. Instead of writing condition notes for 100-500 separate items—burn out imminent!—you can buy in bulk, write a single condition note for the product, set a single price, and ship them with identical labels. This cuts down on the workload and frees you up to continue scaling your business.

Finding that great wholesale product (and then the next great wholesale product) is hard work, but the payoff becomes an inventory that doesn't require a huge amount of time cleaning, prepping, and preparing several items from different categories.

Move Into Private Label

We've discussed private label in great detail in the sourcing products chapter, and while the risks can be high, the same truths apply to private label as wholesale: once you find a great product, the rest of the work with listing is only done a single time. While you will have to develop content, you can outsource some of the work involved in making sales copy convincing and powerful, utilizing great minds to help sell your product. The workload becomes marketing and branding centric instead of hitting the pavement.

The great thing about private label is that you can truly focus on what you love. You can create a community and brand around a hobby or interest you have, and in doing so, the work becomes more enjoyable than trying to sell every single thing under the sun. This one seems very obvious, but it is often overlooked by those tackling the beginner's mentality of going out and finding products to sell. The more you love a product, or the lifestyle around it, the better you will be able to connect with your potential customer in your marketing efforts through your website, blog, social media, etc.

Scaling private label once you have a few successful products becomes easier. As a brand gains recognition for quality and good customer support, putting out new products that reach your market base is going to be the easiest method to continue scaling. There's no reason a successful brand couldn't put out new products several times a year. There's a lot of work involved for each one, but as you grow, affording the help from freelancers becomes less and less of a burden.

Advertise

This works best with private label sales, but it also moves into wholesale and larger distribution models. In the event that you have chosen to specialize in a certain category, it is time to build your platform with that blog, website, social media, and... paid ads!

While this method may not be practical for every solution, paid advertisements through Facebook, Adsense, and Bing Ads are proven to drive large amounts of traffic. With a private label item, some forms of advertising are essential to your success.

The trick about advertising is that it requires testing. Lots of testing. Always create at least two ads for every product you intend to advertise. Test these ads against each other, scrap the one that doesn't work as well, and build a new one to pit against the other.

Dig deep for keywords that are under-utilized by sellers in the same category, and test some more.

If marketing really isn't for you, this process can be outsourced to some extent, but keep in mind that more people touching your business, the more costs involved. In an ideal scenario the rise in profits will justify this, but there is some risk involved.

Learning how to advertise is a huge job unto itself, but taking advantage of the information you have from your reports will help targeting your market a little bit easier.

Improve the Quality of Your Listings

It cannot be stressed that a high-quality listing, especially for private label items or any items where you've created the product page, is going to have a huge impact on the amount of sales you are able to make. If your content is not professional, buyers will write your products off more often than not. By improving the quality of your listings with better condition notes, including images, and writing descriptions for those products you're branding yourself or created a listing for, you're putting professionalism first, and that is not lost on the customer (even if they don't realize it).

Seek Out Reviews

Again, this applies mostly to those with private label products or those that have created product listings for items that are otherwise not available on Amazon. With positive customer reviews comes more customers. It's a proven fact that people respect the word of actual purchasers.

To facilitate an increase in reviews, you will need a method of contacting people that are likely within the market your products land in. If you are private label selling, then you should be developing an online presence, and through this you can offer an item for free in exchange for a review on Amazon. Note that you cannot ask for a positive review; you can simply ask them to give their honest opinion. For this reason, and so many others, you need to make sure that you only sell durable and useful goods.

This method has done a lot for me. Through one of my email lists, I invited people to claim free gifts in exchange for a review on Amazon, a video unboxing, or some other form of honest feedback (and promotion) for the item. All they had to do was send me some proof of their contribution, and they were guaranteed first dibs on the next round of freebies as well. This garnered roughly 20 reviews on Amazon and a few video unboxings on somewhat popular YouTuber channels, and the result was a small rise in sales that helped to increase the reviews more. That item was a success.

Create Bundles

If you're purchasing in wholesale, there's a good chance you're buying products that are similar or even work together quite well. In this event, you are given the ability to create a "bundle" product, create the listing for it, and probably offer a pretty decent deal when considering the prices of the items individually. For example, if you're selling cameras, you can bundle a camera with a carrying case. You could also create an even better bundle that comes with a camera, carrying case, extra lens, and a cleaning kit. If that wasn't enough, you can offer a third bundle option for the same products that also includes a tri-pod. By bundling items, you're offering convenience and a slight discount on the price of items that would often be purchased at the same time anyway.

Bundle listings come with another added benefit. Because you'll have to create the product listing yourself, there won't be other sellers offering the same exact bundle (at least not at first, it is possible someone would try to copy your bundle and use your product listing to sell it). At the same time, this is going to include additional work. Not only will you need to produce the listing's description, you'll need to do so in a way that helps sell the items as a package. Additionally, you'll have to produce the product images, and if you want to be fancy, you may need to produce a demonstration video as well. There are a lot of perks to having this much control over a product that's being sold, but it does incur the extra work.

In the event that you're handling private label items, this process should actually be rather simple. Because you'll already have listing copy written for each item, you can use some of the content that is already created to put together your new product listing. Additionally, you will have total control over the price differences between buying the items separately and buying them together. The great thing is that you can create as many bundle variations as you want without actually buying any new products.

While bundling may not seem like a huge scaling effort, the fact of the matter is that it helps to advertise all of the items, offers obvious value (if priced accordingly), and creates another point of contact with potential customers. If it offers good value, receives good reviews, and typically remains available for sale (not running out of stock often), a bundle can easily become one of your bestselling listings.

Set Goals

One of the most important steps in scaling any business is to set goals and work hard until you reach them. Having a goal leads to the development of a plan, and a plan leads to execution. A realistic goal starting out creates a celebration-worthy milestone in your business. If your goal is to make $1,000 in a month, how many of X products must you buy, and how many must you sell, to reach that goal? As you learn what sells, and thus what to buy, these goals become easier to meet and expand upon.

Keep Records

On a similar train of thought, how can you really plan and expand if you aren't taking the time to keep records of your expenses, earnings, items that sell well, items that sit around too long, etc.? Not only does keeping good records make tax time a heck of a lot easier, but it gives you a full picture of what is working and what isn't. Understanding your business from a mathematical standpoint is a must if you have any expectations of growing it to a sizable income stream. If keeping records is difficult for you, seek out help on accounting.

Take Calculated Risks, Try New Things

This is probably the hardest thing for people looking to scale their Amazon FBA-based businesses, but sometimes if an opportunity arises, it is time to take a chance on it. You should definitely still do your research, but sometimes the window of opportunity is short and hesitating too long means you may have missed out on a golden chance. Not every risk is so huge that it will bankrupt you, even if you do ultimately lose money, and not taking risks means you can expect your profits to taper off. Perhaps $1,000-$2,000 per month is enough for you and the risk seems unnecessary, but very few people have made it big without risking their time, money, and occasionally their peace of mind.

Chapter 11. Avoiding Problems

Unfortunately, you are not the only person selling. You are also not the only person handling your sales, and you are not a perfect human being. Taking into consideration my experience, there are a few problems that could creep up on you that are worth mentioning.

Avoiding Problems

There are a handful of things that are worth NEVER DOING in the Fulfilled by Amazon business. This includes:

1. **Drop shipping…** While it's tempting to find a distributor that is willing to ship directly to Amazon, it is truly best to avoid this. While Amazon allows for this, the major issue is that anything that does go wrong is still considered a ding against you and your account. This means that a huge error on your drop shipping partner's end could be detrimental not only to reviews, sales, and profits, but even to your Amazon account. If you have a partner you have worked with for a long time, you might test the waters out, but the truth is that it's best just to avoid it completely.

2. **Heavy items…** There are some exceptions to this, but for most of us, there is no reason we should be trying to sell anything large in size or extremely heavy in weight. The

shipping costs absurdly high, and that typically leads to lower prices to make up for it on the buyer's end. Low cost items require high volume of sales to be practical, and a high volume of heavy items is just not something you should put yourself through.

3. **Forgetting to charge your smartphone.** This sounds silly, but you are going to be using your cell phone a lot, most specifically during retail arbitrage sessions. If your phone is dead, you can't really use it to scan items in stores to see if they're profitable. Likewise, bring a car charger along with you so you can remedy the situation if you do make this mistake.

4. **Pushing prices down.** Don't do it. While it's tempting to become the lowest price, you should really only be matching prices with the lowest FBA seller. Pushing down the price

leads to further price drops, and soon your profits start to disappear.

5. **Skimp.** This applies to basically everything. Laziness breeds poor results. If you don't clean items, you can get a bad review. If you don't label things correctly prior to shipping, Amazon may not list it. If you write shoddy condition notes or product listings, people will be less interested. One of the reasons it is so possible to create private label products or bundled listings is because a lot of the other people doing the same thing are skimping on content creation and marketing. I'm sure you're groaning at this since I've said it more than once, but CONTENT IS KING. If you skimp, your sales will suffer.

6. **Paying for fake reviews.** This is such a tempting tactic for those with product listings that could use a little boost of attention and love, but never, ever pay for reviews. You can offer people free products in exchange for an honest review, but paying for reviews is a violation of Amazon's terms of services, and they have a habit of shutting down sellers that are caught cheating the system this way.

Solving Problems

Unfortunately, despite any preparation and attention to detail given, there are going to be times where something goes wrong. Some of these things you can't do much about. If the price mysteriously drops on a product and you lose money on it, there's no control on your end to really do anything about that. However, many problems CAN be solved, and here is a list of some common ones that may arise:

1. **Bad reviews.** There's nothing you can do about a bad review on one of your product listings or on your seller account, but if there was a problem that can be fixed on your end, you need to take the time to fix it. If the problem is that an item arrives in pieces, make sure to pad those items better in the future. If

the problem is cheap quality, then it's time to find better products and market them more honestly, which means you NEED decent products because nobody wants to market a piece of crap honestly.

2. **Paid too much for an item.** If you bought something for too much and won't be able to make a profit on it through FBA, there are a few options. If it came from a big box store, you may be able to return it for a refund. If you can't make a profit selling it through Fulfilled by Amazon, you may be able to make a small profit selling it as a merchant fulfilled order instead. If that doesn't work, you can also try to sell it locally. If that doesn't work, you can keep the item and write it off as a business loss.

3. **Lost or damaged shipments to Amazon.** If you have a lost or damaged shipment that was meant for Amazon FBA, then you need to contact that carrier. If you've purchased insurance, then they will likely reimburse you should the package not be found and delivered correctly. One great thing is that Amazon will actually pay for these losses if you use their partner carrier through the Amazon interface. (Currently, there partner is UPS.)

4. **"Unsellable" items.** In this context, an "unsellable item" refers to items that Amazon has marked as unsellable after you've shipped it as part of a package to them. Amazon will send you an alert about this unsellable product, and the reason will

become clear. More often than not, it was simply listed wrong, and you'll need to go into your listing manager and place the item in the right category or something just as simple. Do not fret if you get one of these messages.

5. **"Stranded" inventory.** There are a few reasons items can become "stranded." Sometimes this is because the original manufacturer has removed the product listing. In this event, your course of action is to create a new product listing for this item. If the item has sold well, that may be worth the time, but if it has been sitting around, you can also request that Amazon ships the item back to you or disposes of it.

Hi-jacked Listings, How to Avoid Them, and What to Do About Them

In the last few years especially, it has become popular to begin hijacking listings. By "hijacking" a listing, I am really only suggesting that people are taking listings that you've painstakingly created and selling the item for a little less than you can offer them for, basically stealing all your hard work and marketing efforts in the process. While it is by no means illegal unless it's a private label product and they're claiming to have your brand of product when they really don't, it is shady business acumen. There are a few solutions to this growing problem that will make it easier for you to avoid these hijackers

Difficult to Reproduce Bundles

When creating a new listing, bundle in at least one item that would be difficult (or possibly a little strange) for people to find or source. When doing this, it is smart to make sure the distributor or manufacturer of this extra add-on item is not the same manufacturer of the rest of the bundle. In adding in this unusual or difficult to source item, it becomes absurdly difficult for the listing to get hijacked or even have used sellers. As an example, if you sold a blender, you could add a "free" pig-shaped spatula from another distributor.

Have a Brand Name

Branding your product makes it hard to duplicate, and even if it is easy to duplicate, the type of people hijacking these listings are unlikely to be looking to pay a distributor to brand an item for them. Having these private label items are good in a number of ways, and one of them is that it becomes difficult for a listing to get hijacked.

If your brand becomes well known, knock-offs are possible, so taking the time to file for copyrights and patents that may apply can be helpful in stopping hijackers and bootleggers down the road. Note that any original material is automatically considered copyrighted in the USA, but having proof still makes any legal issues easier.

Don't Mention FBA to Distributors

This sounds a bit strange, but if you're sourcing wholesale goods or your private label products from China, there is something of a threat when they realize that the plan is to simply sell these on Amazon. Distributors may take it upon themselves to sell the same product, especially if you've spoken about the item and your intentions, and that can lead to trouble from the crafty distributor looking for new revenue streams. While you shouldn't be inherently afraid of working with a distributor, it is important to realize that you don't need to provide them with every little bit of information. Ultimately, they could become your competition, and hijacking your listings (whether they realize they are actually your listings or not) is one way that your loose mouth can get you into trouble.

After a Listing gets Hijacked

Unfortunately, it may be too late or someone simply sees the value in your well-produced listings. Someone has hijacked one of your listings, and now you have to decide what you plan to do about it. There are only a few options available here. There's often no reason they CAN'T sell the item (unless it's your brand and they're bootlegging), but sometimes you can put a stop to it or at least lessen the blow.

1. **Drop your prices.** This is probably the last solution anybody wants to hear, but if someone has managed to undercut your price and sales have plummeted as a result, it may be time to drop your price if you can. Making some profit is better than sitting on goods while somebody else makes out like a bandit because of all your hard work and quality control. It's not ideal, but sometimes, it's all you can do.

2. **Request the listing be removed.** This decision is a huge one, but if you take the time to figure out the math, it could potentially earn more money than selling at a lower cost. If you can have Amazon return your product, rebundle it (as per the suggestions above), and ship it back to Amazon for fulfillment through a new listing, you can request that they remove your old listing completely (especially if it's branded). The removal may not always happen, though, so there's a lot of risk involved here. Still, if you can offer the bundle at roughly the same price as before (taking a loss initially, but earning the same once things stabilize), it may be worth the effort.

3. **Catch them cheating.** If you have any reason to believe that those hijacking your posts are not sending the same exact items, you can recruit a friend to buy it from the other seller and report it as a fake or counterfeit product to Amazon. Only report this if it is fake or counterfeit.

4. **Pursue legal action.** Should you have copyright, trademarks, or patents pertaining to the product, threaten the seller with legal actions. Often, just the threat is enough for them to back off and disappear.

It's uncertain if the trend of hijacking product listings will continue to grow, but if it does, these tips and tricks will be vital to making your own product listings safe and hard for hijackers to penetrate. It is sad that you have to protect all of your hard work, dedication, and investments like this, but it is better safe than sorry.

Conclusion

Fulfillment by Amazon is a great opportunity for people looking to work at home, whether the idea is to create an income that surpasses your day job, and allows you to quit, or just fill in your income with some supplemental funds. Despite the high fees and the many details to consider, a smoothly ran FBA approach can become a steam-line cash generator. It can also be a lot of fun if you love to shop, love new challenges, and remember that while you should be serious about your business, negative stress never helps anyone earn more money. You're working for yourself, and that has to be better than sitting in a stuffy office.

Taking the time to learn the process from experienced sellers will shave off a large part of the learning curve, but when it comes down to what you sell and what works best for you, it really is a manner of having some of those learning experiences for yourself. You will make mistakes, but so many times you will also succeed. Fulfillment by Amazon offers those of us that like to play it safe an easy path for selling, but it also provides risk takers with the ability to blow up a product they've created or branded themselves. As Amazon continues to dominate the online marketplace, it is clear that any serious product manufacturer or distributor is going to taking advantage of its platform, and buyers are going to continue to flock to the website and purchase goods. The high level of traffic and trusted history with customers makes it an unparalleled resource for entrepreneurs.

The hard work involved is going to take a lot out of you at times, but the rewards and lessons you reap along the way will make things easier. If you stick to your guns, continue to research and learn, and remain as persistent as possible, you can be one of those people that claim great success with Fulfillment by Amazon. Most importantly, just believe in yourself. You can do this.

Shopify:

Step by Step Guide on How to Make Money Selling
on Shopify

Matthew Scott

Copyright © 2017 by Matthew Scott

Contents

Introduction

Working for yourself in ecommerce is a great way to break away from the nine-to-five grind. It is not without its challenges, and it requires hard work. However, if handled with enthusiasm and dedication, an online shop can become an excellent side hustle or even a full-time gig. The only thing getting in the way of your eventual success is having the guts to take a risk and the fortitude to put in the hard work.

There are many platforms for selling your products online, but for the dedicated seller that wishes to work outside of other marketplaces, such as Amazon and eBay, Shopify is often regarded as the leading choice in all-in-one platforms. Additionally, for the seller that offers products available nowhere else, Shopify becomes one of many ways to sell directly from your own website.

If you're at all on the fence about starting your own ecommerce business, consider the perks:

- You are your own boss. There's nobody to answer to but yourself. For some, that may be a bit daunting, but if you have the skills for self-motivation and maintain high expectations of yourself, you will be able to meet your goals.

- You get to work from home. Don't want to wear pants? Not a big deal. Want to take a break and go out for a beer? Not a problem.

- There's no limit to the amount of profit you can make. You will never hit a salary cap, and your job security will never rely on someone else's decisions. People have left jobs from all income ranges and became absurdly more wealthy on their own than they ever could have in their previous positions; there's no reason you can't do the same.

- You won't get left in the weeds. As small, mom and pop brick-and-mortar stores continue to disappear across the country, online sellers are experiencing the opposite effect. Those with good marketing and great products are thriving by spending far less on overhead and attracting customers from all over the world instead of only catering to a small local area. Even if you do have a brick-and-mortar location, taking advantage of online sales is the only practical way to continue growing your retail business.

- Your shop continues working for you while you sleep. You don't have to man a front desk in order to sell products, and you don't have to get up early every day to make sure someone is there to help the customers. Your shop is always open.

Ecommerce is a great field for budding and serial entrepreneurs, and Shopify makes the process easier by leaps and bounds while offering what most of the other platforms simply don't. Their highly customizable and intuitive design elements completely eliminate the additional cost of having a website designed from scratch, and the platform is produced by a reputable company that has worked out all of the kinks already. Security is already built into your store, so there are very little worries about the potential of customer (or your) information falling into the wrong hands. Additionally, Shopify offers tools that help with marketing and analyzing your sales and profits, and they don't charge any fees for transactions. You only pay a monthly fee that fits the size of your store.

The first step is knowledge, and you're already on your way!

Chapter 1. Required Materials

Before getting started with Shopify, it is wise to take stock of what an ecommerce store will require. The following list will help you check off as much as possible beforehand, but it may not cover everything required for your particular situation. Still, being prepared will save a lot of headache and help you hit the ground running once it's truly time to start your online store.

Time and Work

Unfortunately, nothing worth doing well is going to be quick and easy. Even if you intend to keep your day job while you begin your ecommerce journey, there will be time requirements involved in sourcing products, writing descriptions, taking pictures, marketing your store, communicating with customers, handling shipments, and a myriad of other tasks.

At first, the time investment may only be a few hours a week. However, as you grow your business, the time investment can quickly grow as well. There will be chances to streamline things later, but regardless, you do have to put in the work. Making sure you are able to dedicate time to your shop is vital to your success. If you're already spread too thin, it may be difficult to find the time for ecommerce. It is up to you to decide how much time you can afford to offer your new business.

Capital

While it's true that the cost of opening an ecommerce site is far less than attempting to open a brick-and-mortar operation, you will still need to be able to invest money into your new business while still maintaining your other financial responsibilities and the livelihood of your family. Having some capital on hand is going to ease a lot of your worries starting off. Whether you use credit or dip into your savings, understand that this is a financial risk you are taking, and the decisions you make with your money need to be wise, thought-out decisions.

There is no magic number of dollars you want to start an ecommerce store. This will vary greatly depending on your ambitions, the types of products you aim to sell, and how much money you are able to spend on advertising (if you do spend any money on advertising).

Reliable Technology

This may seem like common sense, but it is important that you have a reliable computer, an internet connection, and potentially a decent DSLR digital camera. Make sure to have a decent printer, plenty of printable shipping labels or plain printer paper, ink, etc. Having these tools will lessen the daily headaches and help you provide the best possible customer experience.

Niche or Target Market

You need a focus. While you can start an online thrift store with every little thing in the world, it is eventually going to be wiser to narrow your store down into a category. This can either be a single product category (cameras, custom shirts and mugs, housewares, etc.) or it can be a specific demographic (millennials, baby boomers, new mothers, etc.). While this isn't exactly a necessity, it is going to go a long way in your success. Providing a full experience for a specific crowd is typically going to be more profitable than attempting to open a supermarket with every little product. You are not WalMart, and attempting to become WalMart on your own is going to almost inevitably become a failed venture. Keeping a broader niche in mind will help make it easier to stock a larger inventory.

Inventory

You have to have something to sell. Sourcing products is going to become a huge part of your new business venture, and we'll cover this in depth in a future chapter. Starting off, it is wise to have at least a small inventory ready to help establish your niche even more.

Shipping Supplies

While you can purchase supplies at the United States Post Office, UPS Store, of FedEx locations, it is wise to procure these in bulk to save money on costs, especially if you are selling many of the same products, as the box sizes will typically be the same for many of them. You will also need tape, those printer-friendly shipping labels (or plain paper), and packing materials such as bubble wrap. It is wise to have a postal scale as well.

Computer Skills

While Shopify minimizes the complications of producing your own website and store, it is important to note that some computer skills are going to make a world of difference. If you can handle email, printing, and basic word processing and spreadsheets, you'll be that far ahead of the game. It helps to have some novice-level understanding of graphic editing, but this isn't something that's going to make or break your business.

Chapter 2. Choosing a Product Category

Before you setup a shop on Shopify, it may be important to consider the types of products you can sell. In ecommerce, there are three basic product categories you can choose from, and Shopify is an excellent platform for all of them.

Digital Products

As you might have guessed, a digital product is something that can be delivered electronically. The largest perk of this product category is that it completely eliminates shipping, dramatically decreasing the time and costs involved in running your ecommerce store. The downside is that digital products often have to be produced, either by the store owner or by contractors. You can sell software from third parties as well, but the market is pretty saturated with this type of thing.

There are a large number of digital products you can sell, and a large part of understanding this market is either improving upon other such digital product concepts or providing something completely new. Some examples of digital products include:

- Sounds samples for musicians and artists to use in their music.

- Software for PC, MAC, etc. This can be software you have developed, or you can work with software developers and offer their products. Note that selling certain software without a license from the company can violate the terms of service of Shopify.

- Web design themes (customizable!)

- Book cover designs (customizable!)

- Other design elements.

- Ebooks, music, and videos. Whether it is instructional ebooks and online courses for surfing or ebooks and movies about high-school aged werewolves on the wrestling team, Shopify is an excellent solution for content creators in need of a sales platform.

- Nearly anything that can be delivered digitally!

Physical Products

Physical products are probably the most common types of products sold through ecommerce, and while the logistics are a lot more involved than digital products, this is likely going to be the path you go down. As long as the product is legal and doesn't violate Shopify's term of services, it can be sold on Shopify.

The upside to physical products is that they are easier to sell. The downside is that you'll have to ship them, handle defective orders and returns, have a place to store them prior to sales, and worst of all, you have to purchase them before you can sell them, making the overhead higher than selling digital goods.

Common physical products include:

- Technology, such as computers, cameras, smart phones, video game consoles, and more.
- Media, such as video games, movies, music.
- Clothing items and accessories
- Beauty products, such as makeup and hair products
- Handmade goods, including customizable clothing and mugs, soaps, one-of-a-kind creations and basically anything you can produce
- Private-label products, which are mass produced products with your own branding on them.
- Pretty much anything.

We'll go into more detail later about how to research what market you want to sell in, how to source products, and alternative methods of handling physical sales, such as drop shipping.

Subscription Products

Subscription products are a rising market as the likes of LootCrate and similar monthly subscription services have exploded in recent years. While there are subscription-specific platforms for selling these types of items, Shopify offers far more tools, customization, customer service, and reliability than these others. Also, there's no reason you can't use more than one platform.

You may have some experience with subscription boxes. There's almost one for everything these days. There's shaving kits that come monthly. There are candy boxes. There are gourmet meat boxes, clothes, video games, movies, collectibles... it is truly endless.

The huge advantage of subscription boxes is that you have an approximation of the amount of product you will require to fulfil your orders because people pay for the product before you even have to assemble the boxes. While you'll likely need to have some product on hand, you can maintain an inventory that makes sense for the amount of subscribers you currently have.

One of the disadvantages is that you need to retain subscribers in order to make this business model work. This means a couple of things for you. First, you'll need to continue to source new products so customers aren't receiving the same things over and over. Second, you need to be able to create a perceived value that exceeds the price you charge. Part of the struggle with subscription boxes is that customers are often disappointed with the offerings for the price, even if they are more than fair considering all of the additional work that goes into putting them together.

With the growth of subscription boxes being offered, it is also worth noting that coming up with an original idea is going to make a huge difference in your success. If the same subscription box you want to curate already exists, the amount of competition can be difficult to overcome. That doesn't mean there isn't room for more strange candy boxes in the world, but it does mean you need to set yourself apart somehow.

As a seller of physical goods, it is obviously possible to sell a subscription box on top of your usual products, and this is a model that many subscription box companies have started to follow through with to hook in customers that may not want the experience of unboxing items they don't truly want but will purchase one or two of the items separately.

Choosing One

You probably have some idea which of these types of product categories you would like to work with. If you are unsure, it is wise to take the time to come up with a general idea for all three, handle some market research, and determine from there which are the most viable, which you are the most passionate about, and how easily the market is to break into. We'll discuss market research in more depth later.

Chapter 3. Legal Concerns

It is worth noting that I am not a lawyer, and the information in this chapter is generalized and should not be considered legal advice. You should check with a law professional to determine if there are any other legal concerns, what applies to your particular situation, and if there are any applicable laws or regulations based on your state of residence. That said, there are a few legal concerns worth considering on your own before you set off on your ecommerce journey or begin paying a legal professional.

Copyright and Intellectual Property

It should go without saying that you must follow all copyright laws when selling products in an ecommerce setup through Shopify. However, there is often some confusion about what is allowed and what falls under the concept "fair use." Let's clear that up.

If you do not own the copyright to a product, trademark, image, or other materials, you cannot utilize it for profit without express permission from the creator or the proper licenses. This especially extends into many areas of design.

An obvious example includes the use of another company or person's intellectual property. Take Nintendo's ever-popular character Mario. Despite the massive amount of products online that use his image, a vast majority of them are technically breaking copyright laws by infringing on Nintendo's trademark character. Without obtaining the proper licensing, placing his image on a t-shirt, mug, poster, notebook, or any other product is technically illegal. This applies even if you drew your own representation of the character. While this type of infringement is often overlooked, it is completely possible for Nintendo to sue you for essentially stealing from them. The same is true for other video game characters, cartoons, movies, etc.

With ebooks, videos, and other digital content, it is obviously copyright infringement to download these items and resell them without first getting permission. Not only is this illegal, but customers tend to frown upon sellers that don't do any of the work for themselves.

Likewise, despite the popular act of simply finding images on Google Images and using them on your design projects, it is crucial that any images you use are either in the public domain or you've paid for a license to use them. This also applies to things like fonts, clip art, design elements, etc. It is a huge misconception that simply because a font may be free to download that it's also free to use for commercial products. If you're not using a font that comes with your computer, it's wise to take the time to determine if you are required to purchase a license to use it. As a rule of thumb, if you're unsure if you're breaking any copyright law, just avoid that particular element, image, etc.

Business Licenses

Not all ecommerce sellers require a business license, but it depends on many factors. First, you should check your state's laws regarding ecommerce and business licenses. Second, if you plan to have any salaried or hourly employees, you will need to obtain a business license and an employer identification number for tax purposes. (It is worth noting that you can hire independent contractors without an employer identification number.)

For those of us that don't need a business license, we will be considered "sole proprietors," and that means that we will generally be the only "employee" in our business. This also means that our personal finances and business finances are intermingled, and as such, our taxes are as well. For this reason, it may be advantageous to obtain a business license even if you don't plan on working with employees. Should you use credit to build your business and have to default on loans or declare bankruptcy, this will be personal bankruptcy instead of business bankruptcy, which will harm your financial health for years to come.

Taxes

As a general piece of advice, you have to pay your taxes.

That said, with online sales, the general rule for federal taxes is that you must claim your earnings in full if you've made more than 200 transactions and netted $20,000 or more in sales. Unless you're still a fledgling seller with a full-time job on the side, it is safe to assume we should just claim our earnings regardless of meeting these criteria.

As mentioned above, if you have employees working under you, you must have an employee identification number, and you must report your employee's earnings. You will be responsible for issuing W-2s for employees. For independent contractors, you will be required to issue 1099-MISC forms if you have paid them over $600 within the year.

It is wise to have a tax professional sit down with you and walk you through all of the ins and outs of taxes as either a business or a sole proprietor. Doing your own taxes may save you a few dollars, but the likelihood of being audited rises dramatically for self-employed individuals that fail to handle the process correctly.

Some states require that you charge sales tax for buyers within the same state as well.

Privacy and Spam

Did you know that it is actually illegal to spam? To put that into perspective, it is illegal to push products in an unsavory way. This doesn't mean you should forego emailing customers; in fact, email lists are a great way to increase sales and market your new products. When you make a sale or if you have someone sign up for an email list, it is alright to email them, you just need to take a few steps to ensure you avoid falling into the "spam" category.

First, all of your messages should be clearly marked as advertisements. Second, the text within the subject line and body of an email shouldn't be misleading whatsoever. Lastly, you need to offer a method for customers to unsubscribe from receiving messages from you. Ideally, you will also include a legal postal address within all of your messages as well, even if it's just a PO Box.

As an online retailer, you're sometimes privy to quite a bit of information concerning your customers, including contact information, postal address, full name, and much more. While it may be tempting to sell this information or use other methods of taking advantage of it, it is highly illegal, and the fines and potential jail time are far more damaging than the meager earnings a bit of scamming offers. Just don't do it.

State Laws

I've mentioned it briefly, but it is important to understand that some states have their own laws regulating how ecommerce and running a business in that state must be handled. Take the time to research your state laws, talk with legal professionals, and make sure to utilize this knowledge to avoid potential issues.

Reminder!

This is not a complete list of legal issues, but it is a brief starting off point to help you avoid the most common legal mistakes new entrepreneurs find themselves making. It is highly advised to seek legal consul and do your own research regarding the potential legal issues surrounding your business.

Chapter 4. Market Research

Taking the time to do market research can help in many ways. Not only can help you determine if your great idea is indeed profitable, but it can help you discover your target audience, come up with new products to create or source, and save you from making costly mistakes trying to promote and sell products that are unlikely to be popular with customers. In taking the time to do your market research, you are getting ahead of the competition by learning about the market and the major players in the market.

What's Already Available?

An excellent place to start is to consider what is already available within the market. There are many ways to do this. This most obvious place to start is going to online retailer platforms and browsing through some of the bestselling items in the category you aim to sell in.

For example, if you plan to sell microphones, it would be wise to take the time to look through Amazon's top-selling microphones, and then pinpoint that further as much as you can. What microphone sells the best for recording vocals? What microphone sells the best for recording instruments? What USB microphones are common for podcasting, and which USB microphones are the most common for Skype and other non-professional applications?

Understanding what already sells helps you understand which products to pick and what to work on when developing a product, should you choose to go that route.

Another thing you can learn from Amazon product pages is what items people regularly buy with other products. Going back to the microphone example, you might notice on the product page for the Shure SM57 (a popular dynamic microphone for musicians) that people also tend to purchase the XLR cables required to use the microphone, a microphone stand, a microphone preamp, etc. Just having an idea of all the products that fall within your niche will help you continue to expand your inventory as your store grows.

Sticking with this example, if you were to consider developing a microphone or creating a private label product with a mass produced microphone that you can print your branding on, you can learn from customer reviews which features and attributes of the product customers like or don't like. Taking all of these details into account will help you meet the needs of your target demographic and reduce the likelihood of sourcing products nobody wants.

Amazon also helps you get an idea of the prices people are willing to pay for the item you're trying to sell. Trying to sell much higher than Amazon is sometimes difficult unless you somehow provide something that a normal purchase off of Amazon cannot provide, even if that is through your other platforms and not the store itself.

Additionally, if you have a particular product you're considering selling, then you can find this item on Amazon and see its sales rank. If the sales ranking is very low (a high number), it may not be a viable seller for you. There's little use in selling products that are widely available if nobody is really buying them. This is an easy way to eat away at your capital before you even really get started.

Leaving Amazon, we can also learn from taking a look at other retailers. Look for your competition. If you have a shop called "Music Lover's Round Table," then it might be wise to take the time to understand who else is servicing the same niche. This particular niche is pretty saturated, but if you can provide some type of solution to a problem, all niches with an audience can become a viable option. What about your competition is favorable or unfavorable to your customers, and what can you do to avoid the same pitfalls or copy and exceed their successes?

Taking the time to learn about the competition is key to your success, especially in some of the smaller niches where it's logistically possible for a one-person business to overcome the competition. Leaving the stores, you can also stalk your competition on social media, their website and blogs, and on review websites. The more you can learn from people that have gone before you, the better.

Keyword Research

In a subsequent chapter, we are going to talk about keyword research and how it applies to improving your store's visibility in search engines and how to target paid advertisements. This market research, however, will lay the ground work for those tasks. Additionally, you'll be able to learn about your market simply by understanding the search habits of your prospective customers.

The first thing you can do is simply run a quick Google search for the types of products you want to sell and see what comes up. Google's search bar will also show you some similar search terms along the way, and it is often wise to take the time to look these over as well. Largely, this is going to show you what type of content people are seeing when they search for the same thing. Once again, it gives you a chance to size up the competition, and it also helps give some ideas about what you can do to improve upon what's already available to everyone.

Taking this much further, I want you write down a list of keywords and phrases that apply to the type of products you want to sell, common topics surrounding your market, and specific product names. I would type this list up so you can easily copy and paste later.

Next, it's time to use these words by taking advantage of Google's Keyword Planner. This tool is designed to help you create ads and appropriate bids for these ads on Google Adwords, the advertisement service that Google offers and uses on its own search results. You can get enough information without actually opening any ad campaigns to make this worth your while.

In Google's Keyword Planner, type in the keyword you have in mind, and it will pull up quite a bit of information. This software offers suggestions for related keywords, information on how often the keywords have been searched within a month, and a generalized idea of how much people are paying to place ads that show up when these keywords are typed into a search bar or are related to the page they're displayed on.

This data is valuable for many reasons. It is not going to show you a direct number of sales or how much money people are spending on any particular product or category of products, but it will help you understand if a market or product is trending, if people are actively seeking information or products by using these keywords, and just how competitive it is. While a high competition rate through the Keyword Planner doesn't mean you won't sell a certain product or can't break into a certain niche, it does mean that people will have a harder time finding this product on your ecommerce store through Google.

It is wise to write down those keywords and key phrases that have low competition and a moderate to large amount of searches per month. If possible, it is ideal to incorporate these keywords and key phrases into your product titles and descriptions in an organic manner. We'll discuss this more later, but write these down while you're at it, and keep them somewhere you'll remember to find them later.

If you're unsure of the direction you aim to go with your ecommerce business, keyword research may be the best starting off point. If you can find a niche with large amounts of searches but low amounts of competition, that suggests that the competition isn't spending a lot of money on advertising these products, which makes it easier for you should you go that route. Additionally, it generally suggests that you will have the possibility of becoming one of the first-page results when people type in this particular phrase or word. Many entrepreneurs have used Keyword Planner and similar tools to pinpoint untapped niches in the past, and despite the growth of ecommerce over the last ten years, it is still possible to find a market that hasn't been completely saturated.

Another great thing about this type of keyword research is that it can help you name your shop, your domain name (.com address), and products with keywords that work well within search engines.

Surveys

The third method of learning about your potential market and the people that belong within your niche is to start asking them. Seems obvious, right? Using paid survey services, you can offer small monetary compensation for people's opinions. You will need to formulate useful questions, but learning as much as possible about the demographic that's interested in the type of products you aim to sell, the brand you aim to build, or the services you hope to offer is a great way to save yourself from wasting time.

If you're a little bit tech savvy, I suggest the use of Amazon's Mechanical Turk (MTurk.com) for sourcing survey results. With this tool, you can use Google Forms to build a survey, post a "HIT" (human intelligence task), and have people answer your survey questions in a rather quick way. The great thing is you can limit responses to USA only if that is the market you expect.

If setting up a survey and handling payments to respondents sounds like a daunting task, there are providers on Fiverr.com that will handle this for as low as $5 per 100 responses. Additionally, professional survey services like SurveyMonkey.com offer targeted demographic research and survey fulfilment. It is going to cost more, but the results will also be better tailored to your needs.

If you have a website, blog, social media account, or other platform with a decent amount of followers, it is also possible to simply post your survey on these to bring in responses from those that are most likely to be your first customers. Taking advantage of your network is a great way to start, just keep in mind that "friends and family" aren't your target market.

Putting It Together

While this market research doesn't guarantee you success, it will paint a much clearer picture of the demographics you aim to serve, and it will help you understand what the competition is doing. Likewise, understanding your line of products better is going to make it much easier to help customers get the very best experience possible when shopping through your website. This market research will also be helpful when you begin branching out into blogs, social media, and other methods of promoting your business. Not only will you understand the customers better, but you'll have already completed the first steps that go into creating excellent content tailored toward search engines.

It is vital that you don't skip the market research stage. This is a common mistake, and a huge one, because those that fly by the seat of their pants are often hit hard with the realization that they've invested hundreds or even thousands of dollars into purchasing a product that will never sell fast enough, or they've walked themselves into a niche that simply doesn't have enough paying customers to be viable as a full-time source of income. In fact, market research is so important that even after you've conducted it and found some success at your new venture, you should continue your market research to keep on top of what is trending in your niche, what is happening within the competitive realm of paid advertising, and what new products may be available.

Market research is a perpetual asset if you just stay on top of it. If your business grows to the point where you simply cannot afford the time to handle market research and all of the other tasks, you can hire a freelance contractor online through sites like Upwork.com to handle market and keyword research on your behalf.

Once you have your market research completed (for now), and you've decided to pull the trigger on a specific niche or set of products... it's time to begin sourcing those products.

Chapter 5. Sourcing Your Products

Without the right products to sell, your Shopify shop and ecommerce goals cannot become the money earning potential you're expecting. The process of sourcing new products and determining if they are going to be viable for your store can be a difficult road to travel. This is especially true when you're just starting out, as the amount of capital on hand is probably limited. However, once fruitful sources of great products are secured, it becomes much easier to scale up your business and earn greater profits. There are several sources for products you can sell through your ecommerce website.

Used Goods

A simple place to start is with used goods. Unlike new goods, used goods are easy to find at a very steep discount. However, it is often difficult to continue finding the same products if it isn't something wildly popular. For this reason, it is typically suggested to offer both used goods and new goods if used goods are an avenue you intend to go down at all. If you only offer used goods, just keep in mind that you may be spending a lot of time on writing product descriptions, taking pictures, and posting your products. The issue here is that you're putting in a ton of time to sell only one item that's available.

From there, all of that content generation work is simply going to waste. That said, there are certain niches where selling used goods is going to be highly profitable, and likewise, even if you sell new goods, having a used option at a discount may help secure additional business.

You can source used goods from a number of places, including:

- **Your home.** Starting a store is a decent way to clean out some clutter, especially as a way to get used to the Shopify format.

- **Yard sales.** These are a great opportunity for cheap goods. If you go this route, frequently attending multiple per weekend is the key to finding great deals.

- **Flea markets.** As with yard sales, going frequently and to as many locations as possible increases your odds of finding something great. Likewise, being friendly and making connections is a great way to build a network of people that are willing to give you good deals in the future.

- **Craigslist.** If you live in a large city, Craigslist free section may help you get started with your business. You can also browse what's for sale and post wanted ads.

- **Facebook buy/sell/trade groups.** These are great because, unlike Craigslist, it takes some of the guess work out of determining if someone is safe to deal with, and it makes it a lot easier to make long-lasting connections with people.

If the product or niche you are servicing is highly open to used goods in great condition, it may be advantageous to take the time and put out feelers. These feelers, essentially ads, are appropriate for Craigslist and Facebook groups. You can directly advertise the items you are looking to buy, how much you are willing to pay, and how quickly the pay can be in the seller's hand. For example, if I were focused on selling cell phones, MP3 players, and similar electronics, it would fairly simple to write a post on Craigslist or Facebook, or other online classifieds for that matter. It may read something like this:

BUYING IPHONES, IPODS, and OTHER ELECTRONICS

Need quick cash now? Have an extra cell phone? I'll come to you, test your phone, and pay you within 24 hours! Just PM me for details!

iPhone 7 - $200

iPhone 6 - $100

iPod Touch (6th Gen) - $75

These prices are just examples, but you get the idea. In general, it is wise to purchase items at a third of the cost you want to sell them at. For some, because Shopify doesn't have the types of fees you see from eBay and Amazon stores, it is possible to pay a little bit more and make a decent profit on items that move quickly. These types of ads can be spread out across multiple channels and posted fairly frequently, just be sure to follow any rules laid out by those moderating the channels where you're offering to buy.

One word of caution is that trying to pay low prices locally inherently brings about the likelihood of negative criticism. Do not engage in flame wars. If someone questions your methods or prices, engaging them will only make you look like you have something to hide or deserve that criticism. It makes you look dumb.

Again, the problem with used goods is that each sale may require the time and effort that goes into creating high-quality listings, and this method may not be worth it for many niches.

Retail Arbitrage

New goods can be sourced in practically all the ways you can source used goods, but there are other outlets as well. The next common method for new sellers with limited capital is to take advantage of retail arbitrage. Arbitrage is essentially walking into a store, buying products that are priced lower than they can be sold online, and then reselling them. This method is popular amongst Amazon sellers, but it can work for some Shopify sellers as well. The easiest way to determine the viability of these items is to check their prices against Amazon. If you can buy it for a third of the cost it sells for on Amazon, you can very likely make a profit on it once someone has paid for it. To help keep an item from sitting around, it is also wise to use Amazon to check how popular the item is. If the item is a bestseller on Amazon, there's obviously no worries about trying to sell it. However, Amazon provides information near the bottom of product pages that tells us how well the product sells on their site. The lower the sales rank, the better the odds of making a sale if priced fairly. I prefer to keep products under that 100,000 mark. However, if you're in a niche business, then it may be viable to sell certain products that fall outside of this range. For these, consider the ratings of products that are within the smaller categories on Amazon that best apply to your product.

Once again, because this method doesn't offer items in bulk too often, it may require additional work on your part when listing products. This makes scaling your business difficult and continues to add to the workload.

Wholesale

Wholesale is the epitome of the tried and true cliché of "buy low, sell high." Because you're committed to such a large number of each product you sell, the manufacturer or supplier is going to offer a discounted rate per unit. You can then sell the units individually.

Making wholesale worthwhile involves taking the time to determine which products are going to be viable for you to sell; a bad decision in purchasing is going to lead to a lot of product sitting around in your house or storage units. Products that don't move mean a huge financial loss. This is why market research is so important. Do not buy anything in wholesale amounts on a whim.

With literally thousands of wholesalers in the industry, it may be a surprise to learn that the top 50 wholesale distributors make up almost a quarter of the profits. The best wholesale opportunities are not simple to walk into and require some hard work and networking before you can get killer deals on great products. This doesn't mean a new seller can't break into the wholesale game, but it does mean that you have to be prepared to work for the best opportunities.

Often, a wholesaler is not a manufacturer. The manufacturer will produce the items, and then they sell them in huge amounts to wholesalers. The wholesalers then sell to you in bulk, but still in much smaller amounts. In some cases, the wholesaler is actually just facilitating sales, and you will actually receive items direct from the manufacturers while paying more for them because the wholesaler is the one that made the sale.

When it is possible to work specifically with a manufacturer, the prices are going to be highly in your favor, but this only happens once you have the capital and know-how to purchase and sell large amounts of a single product. Building these types of relationships with wholesalers and suppliers is possible through trade shows, leveraging contacts you make over time, and simply earning the respect of those in charge.

Because you haven't had the opportunity to build these relationships, you will most likely need to work with wholesalers that are open to selling smaller amounts and aren't able to offer the best possible discounts. Don't let that stop you from going the route of wholesale, however, as there are still plenty of resources available even for new ecommerce sellers on Shopify.

To find wholesales, consider the following methods:

- **"Ask and you might receive."** One method of finding a decent wholesaler is to find other retailers that offer the same type of items you intend on selling. From there, you can email them and ask for a recommendation. While some sellers may be threatened if you are their competitor, others may offer you this information in good faith. It is my recommendation that if you expect this type of help from your competition, you should later be willing to reciprocate if anyone asks you for similar information. That's just good karma.

The ideal situation is to find retailers that have a similar market but wouldn't be your DIRECT competition. For example, if you were aiming at selling RC Cars for hobbyists (i.e. gas powered remote controlled cars), you might find a retailer that sells drone-related goods and ask them if they have any recommendations. From there, you can determine if their suppliers are also selling stuff in your niche. These types of communications can lead to long-lasting relationships where both parties can benefit each other.

If someone tells you to take a hike, then don't press the issue. You have more important things to work on.

- **Online directories** can lead you to hundreds of wholesale opportunities. While these may not provide items as cheaply as a close relationship with a supplier, it is a good starting off point for many sellers, especially those that have taken the time to do their market research, understand and reach their target audience, and are willing to put in the time to demonstrate the products and write excellent content. Popular wholesale directories include:
  - https://www.doba.com/
  - http://www.wholesalecentral.com/
  - http://alibaba.com
  - http://salehoo.com

- **Trade shows** will usually have more than one wholesaler present, and after talking to a representative, you may be given some insight into how they operate, if they fit your markets, etc. Likewise, you can network with other retailers in your niche or niches that relate to similar markets and ask for their advice. Being willing to connect with others in commerce will become a huge asset if you're a people person.

It is important to note that not all wholesale directories and companies are safe to work with. It is always wise to take at least a few minutes to do some basic research about a company before you attempt to do business with them. While some young companies may be great partners, it is wise to go through services (such as those listed above) that generally take the time to verify that their suppliers are indeed legitimate operations that will ensure good customer experiences. As a newcomer to ecommerce, it is wise to work with people that have some type of feedback and reputation within the industry. At this point, risking capital to save a few bucks is not wise.

Wholesale will be a huge part of doing business in a streamlined manner. Unlike selling items one at a time, having a bulk of several products allows for your hard work in content creation, marketing, and product sourcing to pay off. For this reason, going wholesale is highly recommended. It may be easier to start with a smaller setup, but large volume should eventually be the goal.

Smaller Lots

While I've pushed you toward buying wholesale via wholesalers, it is also possible to purchase items in bulk via eBay, other auctions, and even locally. The great thing about eBay as a resource starting out is that it is essentially a retail marketplace, so those that do sell in bulk are usually willing to sell in lower volumes. While this means you may not get as great of a deal per unit, it also means you can test out products and how well they will sell without purchasing hundreds of them at a time first. If a product that sells wholesale on eBay does seem viable, you can either try to find another supplier or attempt to work out a deal with wholesalers on eBay for a better rate if you buy a certain amount of a product.

How to Keep Up?

As we've discussed, wholesale is excellent for making your work pay off several times over, but it also comes with its many risks and drawbacks. Aside from determining if a product is viable for the market, buying and selling in large volumes brings up two major concerns for ecommerce entrepreneurs:

- **How do I store these items?**

  You may have to give up your garage or rent a storage unit. If this isn't an option, stay tuned for a better solution...

- **How will I handle large volumes of sales, customer service, and shipping all by myself?**

  This is the question! Once you are successful, how do you continue to scale, or even just handle what you already have, without working yourself to death?

The answer to both of the questions is the dropshipping method. Dropshipping is essentially allowing manufacturers or wholesalers to ship the item to your customer on your behalf. While profits per unit will be significantly lower through dropshipping, the sheer volume you can handle without actually storing, packaging, and shipping your products is going to allow for much better scaling, which usually results in better profits. Additionally, most dropshippers won't require you to actually buy anything in bulk upfront, saving capital for better investments.

The dropshipping method is easily the best way to scale a large ecommerce business through Shopify, and as such, we will cover it in much greater detail in Chapter 9. For now, we will continue to consider other methods of sourcing products.

Private Label

Private label is essentially the same as going the route of wholesale in terms of receiving a product, but you are also going to be branding items. This is wise when you are working in a niche that has room for new brands. A niche like digital cameras is probably not viable due to giants like Nikon and Canon, but a smaller niche like hobbyist-level kites may actually have room for new players. (Don't quote me on that.)

The major difference with wholesale and private label is that you are likely going to work with a manufacturer directly. They will have usually already developed the product you're interested in selling, but you are going to have it branded with your logo, and possibly adjusted in a few other ways. The brand becomes as much of the product as the item itself. Without promoting the brand in a way that it catches on, the product itself may not sell well. Branded products in the private label realm are a huge risk if you're not excellent at marketing.

Production

For those of us that have created a product and can produce it ourselves or have another manufacturer produce them on our behalf, the route of Shopify as our main interface for selling is intelligent. With production comes a lot of legal concerns, such as how to protect your intellectual property, making sure it is safe, and making sure you advertise it in a way that isn't considered fraudulent. I'd assume most creators with a viable product are able to answer all of these questions wisely.

The great thing about production is that there's typically no direct competition. Nobody else should be selling the exact product you have developed, and if you can gain tractions on your product, it can literally blow up into something huge.

Production takes many forms. For those of you that wish to sell digital products, production may be writing books, producing online video courses, working on software, etc. In the event that you can handle every part of the process yourself, production becomes an extremely viable option for sourcing products. It requires certain skills, or at least the ability to generate excellent ideas and put together a team that can execute them. However, digital products are especially high in return once they begin selling. There is such a small cost involved in delivering the product that once you make back the cost of development, the rest is just profit in your pocket. You aren't spending time packing boxes! This route isn't for everyone, and the internet is flooded with content providers like this, but it goes to show that innovative ideas aren't only new physical goods.

Diversify!

The great thing is that you really don't have to stick to one of these methods. You can easily integrate several of them depending on the opportunities available to you at the time, the product research you've done to determine what is viable for sale, and simply the amount of capital available. If you produce a product but also want to sell items that fit the same market, there's no reason you can't offer both. Diversifying, especially at first, may be the best way to find out what works BEST for you. If you ultimately land on product development due to success of your previous products, then that's great! You can further diversify by selling that same product through other channels. If wholesale makes you all of your income, then it is easy to start focusing on that. However, if you find success in multiple approaches, you can always continue to diversify.

The important thing about product sourcing is that you stay on top of it. In a healthy ecommerce experience, you will need to be ready to release new items for sale fairly often to keep your return customers happy. You want return customers, and you definitely want them to be happy! If there's never anything new to buy, then there's one less reason to come back.

As I promised before, we will discuss dropshipping in getter detail in a later chapter. For now, I believe it is best for you to start understanding how Shopify works! Let's jump in!

Chapter 6. Setting Up Your Shopify Store

Are you ready to actually open your Shopify store? Take your time when handling this, making sure all information is typed in correctly, you understand the costs involved, and that you explore your options thoroughly.

Which Shopify Plan Suites You

Shopify offers a free 14-day trial, and it is generally wise to take advantage of this while initially setting up your store so you have a chance to become comfortable with the platform. However, it is not a free service, and you will eventually have to pay for a plan that best suits your needs before your store and website actually goes live on the internet.

All plans come with unlimited product listings, shipping discounts (which get better as you upgrade plans), and no transaction fees when payments are handled with Shopify Payments.

At the time of this writing, Shopify offers the current plans:

Shopify Lite

Cost: $9 per month.

Credit card transaction fees: 2.9% of sale plus 0.30 cents per transaction for online sales, 2.9% of sale and no additional cost for in-person sales.

Shopify Lite only offers "Point of Sale" support. Point of sale essentially suggests a "Cart"-style setup, the great safety features of Shopify, custom invoice creation, and a "buy button." Lite also offers integration into Facebook. This option is really only good if you already have a dedicated website that you intend to sell through. It is typically not advised for those new to ecommerce for one main reason: the costs involved in creating a fully-functioning ecommerce website, even with Shopify's cart and product management, is likely to far outweigh the costs of using a better plan.

Some of the features include:

- Fraud analysis (to prevent fraudulent purchases)
- Integration into Facebook
- Unlimited file storage for images and digital products
- The ability to generate discount codes that can be used for marketing purposes.

Shopify Basic

Cost: $29 per month

Credit card transaction fees: 2.9% of sale plus 0.30 cents per transaction for online sales, 2.7% of sale and no additional cost for in-person sales.

Third-party payment transaction fees: 2.0%

Shopify's Basic Plan offers a wide range of some of the best offerings they have for a fairly small cost of only $29 per month. It includes everything found in the Lite plan, plus many other great perks. This includes:

- **Website and blog.** One major reason to choose this over the Lite plan is that their website and blog building platform is including in the cost, removing a huge amount of cost involved in designing and implementing your own website solutions into your ecommerce goals.

- **Integration into most social media platforms**, should you choose to attempt to incorporate point of sale into your social media.

- **Staff accounts**, two total, to allow others to work together with you on your ecommerce website. Staff accounts allow you to limit the control and information employees can gain when handling business for you, making it safer to work with team members when they are not co-owners. This is especially true if you work with contractors, as you may not even know these people on a personal level.

Other than these two major inclusions, the Basic plan is essentially the Lite plan. That may sound like very little for the additional $20 a month, but if you add up the cost of website design and hosting, it is easily a better solution for the vast majority of applications. Additionally, because Shopify's blog and website features are user friendly, it doesn't require the constant need to either learn how to design your own website or hire someone to handle the webmaster role on your behalf.

Shopify (Standard)

Cost: $79 per month

Credit card transaction fees: 2.6% of sale plus 0.30 cents per transaction for online sales, 2.5% of sale and no additional cost for in-person sales.

Third-party payment transaction fees: 1.0%

Shopify's standard plan (referred to simply as "Shopify"), has all the great features you see in the Basic Plan, and it adds the following:

- **Five staff accounts** for your larger team to help you with your ecommerce solutions.

- **Better shipping discounts** than the Basic Plan.

- **The ability to sell gift cards to your store**, making it possible to earn more profit through the opportunity of loved ones, friends, and businesses to dispense gift cards to potential customers that are specifically made for your shop.

- **Professional reporting tools** that make it easier to understand what is working and what isn't working within your ecommerce store.

- **Abandoned cart recovery!** This means that if someone leaves your website before they actually purchase anything that they've put into their shopping cart, those items will remain should they visit your website again. This may seem like it's not a big deal, but statistics tell us that roughly 14% of customers add items to the cart and get as far as the checkout screen. From there, only 4% actually tend to place an order at all! With more than half of shopping carts going abandoned completely, the ability for a customer to return to your store and see the items they previously considered can dramatically improve your sales. If the customer already has their contact information stored, you can even go into Shopify and send a reminder to them to give them a second chance to check out!

Shopify Professional

Cost: $299 per month

Credit card transaction fees: 2.4% of sale plus 0.30 cents per transaction for online sales, 2.4% of sale and no additional cost for in-person sales.

Third-party payment transaction fees: 0.5%

The Professional Plan allows for all the great features we've discussed, but for the high volume seller, it can add additional savings and features. This includes:

- **Fifteen staff accounts** for larger companies with many employees.
- **Even better discounts on shipping labels.**
- **Advanced report building tools** to help you truly analyze your Shopify business from top to bottom, allowing you to make the best decisions possible as your business begins to scale up.
- **The ability to include third-party calculated shipping costs for customers prior to checkout.** This makes it much easier to provide multiple shipping options. Giving the customers a preference makes it more likely that they will push the final checkout button!

Which One to Choose?

Although it offers the most features, the Professional Plan is only worth it for those selling in extremely high volumes that can justify the $299 per month cost. At high volumes, the discounted credit card and third party payments, along with the additional discounts on shipping, will shave off some of the cost involved in operating your business. For most people starting out, the Basic Plan offers enough to get them off their feet without taking away important capital from the business. You can always upgrade plans later, so once it's viable for you to move up, it will be a piece of cake to get those extra perks.

Starting Your Account

Getting started with Shopify is a fairly painless process. You can start by signing up for your account and a free 14-day trial by navigating to http://shopify.com. On the front page is a textbox asking for your email address to get started.

Just type in your email address and press "Get started" to begin.

The following screen will ask you for a password and the name of your store. You can change the store name later, but it is best to lock it early in your ecommerce journey. To change this later, simply go to the "Settings" link on the main store dashboard after you log into your account.

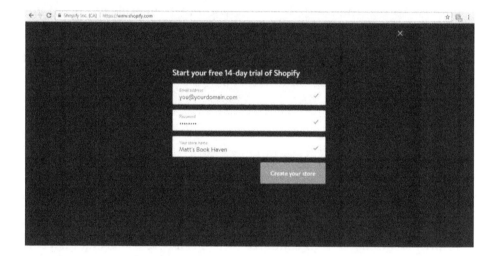

The following set of pages will ask for a handful of information. This includes your legal name, address, and a few questions about your business. Once you've answered these simple questions, Shopify will generate your store, and your 14-day free trial will begin. You can select a plan as soon as you've started, but I suggest playing around with the features a bit first.

That's all there is to setting up your account! You'll need to add more details later, but for now, you can begin learning how to use the interface.

The Shopify Interface

Immediately after signing up, you are brought to the dashboard interface for your store, site, and blog. In this interface are all the tools you need to succeed with creating and managing your Shopify store. Let's take a look at some of the features.

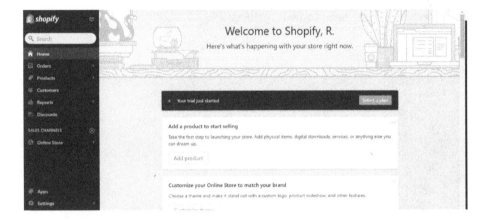

Search Bar

At the top of the interface's navigation, you'll see a search bar. This can be used to find practically anything related to your store and site. You can search for products, customers, and blog posts that you've written simply by typing in some relevant keywords and pressing the return key.

Home

The home link will bring you back to the page you see when you first logged in. This works regardless of which page you have navigated to.

Orders

As you can see in the image below, the "Order" link brings up a new page and several new menu options.

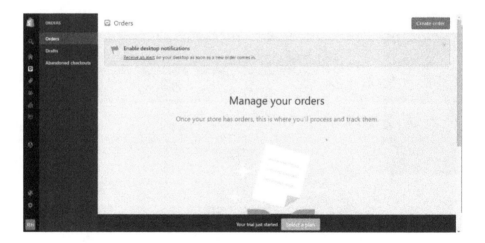

The "Orders" link brings you back to the main page where all orders are displayed. This is the easiest way to keep track of your orders. You can also activate desktop notifications from this page, making it so your computer lets you know when new orders have come in.

Note that you will receive email notifications by default, so you may opt out of this additional desktop notification.

The "Drafts" link allows you to draft invoices and custom orders for your customers and clients.

The "Abandoned Checkout" link will show you those carts that people have left without checking out. If the person has went far enough along in the buying process, you will have the option to send them a notification about their abandoned cart in hopes of reeling them back in. Keep in mind that this tool is only available for the Shopify (Standard) and Professional plans.

Products

Going back to the main navigation bar, the "Product" link brings you to a page that lists all of your products, allows you to add new products, manage inventory, and view the analytics available on your products.

Customers

The "Customers" page is a crown jewel for ecommerce platforms. Unlike many other platforms where they're technically facilitating the sale on your behalf, Shopify gives you actual access to customer information ranging from their names, to their purchases, and even their location. The information provided here is invaluable for market research and outreach to past customers. For example, if you notice an influx of sales from one particular location, you may want to spend time marketing to that location in hopes of increasing your traction within that region.

Reports

The "Reports" page is another invaluable resource. This is another one of Shopify's huge perks over other ecommerce platforms; their robust reporting tools help paint a clear picture of what is working for your business. You won't have anything to look at here until things pick up, but the intuitive design makes it easy to run reports on several criteria. These criteria include:

- Sites that referred visitors
- Devices used by store visitors
- Location of visitors
- An analysis of shopping habits, what people put in their carts, etc.
- Payment methods used
- Sales by month, week, day, hour, etc. Using this analytical tool makes it easy to pinpoint if new marketing advances are indeed driving in new sales.
- Tax reporting
- Many, many more criteria.

Discounts

Finally, the "Discounts" link is where you work on creating promo codes and reward programs for your customers. These tools are excellent sources to help marketing reach a little bit further and encourage return customers to continue shopping at your store. You are also able to actively monitor how these codes are used to assess their usefulness. There are several types of discounts you can offer:

- Percentage discounts, where a specific percentage is taken off their final price. These are great for boosting sales.

- Dollar amount discounts work almost like gift card codes, and they allow you to take a very specific amount off of an order. A $10 code can easily be passed around to encourage new buyers or return customers to add a couple items to their cart. You can limit these dollar amount discounts to work only when a certain charge is reached (i.e. $10 off purchase of $40 or more). You can also apply it to a single product or product category if desired, and if that wasn't enough, you can produce promotional codes for individual customers!

- And there's the free shipping discount that takes off all shipping costs at the end of checkout. This is customizable to apply only to certain locations (i.e. US-only) and certain dollar amounts in sales (i.e. free shipping on orders over $99).

In addition, all promotional codes can be setup so they only work a certain number of times. For instance, you can set up a promotion where the first 50 customers to use the code receive 25% off their entire order. Once 50 people have claimed the code, it will no longer be valid. No need to manually delete it when the promotion ends!

Online Store

Going back to the navigation bar, the link for "Online Store" brings you to a navigation menu that helps you setup your online store. This page also shows how to customize your website. This is where you can apply pre-designed themes, start your blog, and setup your website. We'll come back in Chapter 10 for a full run-through of all the features.

Apps

Moving back to the main navigation menu, near the bottom is the "Apps" link. This is where you can add and edit all of your apps integrated into your website and store. These apps are a great way to expand the functionality of your website, and its highly encourage that you spend some time digging through them. A few apps may already come preinstalled based on your theme, but you can also go through the "App Store" to find free and paid apps to improve your overall design. We will cover a handful of useful tools found in the App Store during Chapter 10.

Settings

The final piece of the main navigation menu is "Settings." Let's run through this section now in order to finish setting up your Shopify store. The sections include:

- General – this is where you input your store name, change your email address, put in the legal street address for your business, and input your time zone and measurement standards.

- Payments – This is where you can setup the payment methods accepted at your store. It is my advice to offer at least the main three payment methods (Shopify Payments, PayPal, Amazon Payments), so run through each setup quickly when you have the chance. If you don't have a PayPal or Amazon Payments account, I suggest getting them.

- Checkouts – In this page of the settings, you have many options regarding the way the customer's experience the checkout experience. You can opt for all checkout to be handle as guests (meaning people will always have to input them information), opt for customers to be required to have a buyer's account on your store (not suggested for most stores), or allow the customer to use either option. There are many other checkboxes here, but it is typically going to be wise to leave them at their default settings and move to the bottom of the Checkouts screen. You'll see three large textboxes where you can enter your return policy, privacy policy, and terms of service. Do not skip these. Even generic ones are better than nothing. If you're unsure, you can use the buttons next to these boxes that reads, "Generate sample," and edit it to fit your needs.

- Shipping – This is where you change your shipping address and the shipping options for your customers. Additionally, this is where you enable third-party shipping, and if you're working through a dropshipper, you can also enable this here. Keep in mind that third-party shipping requires a Professional plan.

- Taxes – This is where you'll enter all your sales tax information. For most of us, there's no need to change anything on this page, but it is important to check your state laws regarding ecommerce business.

- Notifications – You can customize the email notifications customers receive from every step along the path of their purchase. This includes order confirmation, cancellations, refunds, and abandoned carts. This is also where you setup notifications for shipping, whether that's to the customer or to the third-party fulfilment service that handles the delivery of products for you. Additionally, you can standardize customer account notifications used to contact customers for any other reason. Lastly, you can setup notifications to be sent to your email or through desktop notification for real-time information regarding orders and shipments.

- Files – This is where you'll want to upload any images or videos that are relevant to your blog or your product descriptions. Remember, all tiers of the Shopify service come with unlimited file storage, so take advantage of it! Adding in files here will make them available elsewhere. When adding in images elsewhere throughout Shopify, they should also become available within this page.

- Sales Channels – If you intend to integrate Shopify into social media sales, Amazon sales, or any other sales channel, this is where you set that up. There's a ton already available, and most of the ones that aren't initially on the page are accessible by using a Shopify app designed specifically for it.

- Account – Finally, the account settings is where you'll see an overview of your account, be able to add in your credit card to pay for your monthly service, and manage staff accounts. Additionally, you'll be able to monitor the invoices and fees from Shopify that are due or have been paid in the past. This is also where you would close your store, or just pause it while you're on vacation and cannot process orders.

Take your time through the settings pages and take advantage of all the customization available. A customized experience that's aimed specifically at your target market is going to do wonders for customer retention! We'll discuss more customization in Chapter 10.

That's it for the basic Shopify interface! As you can tell, it's laid out in an extremely user-friendly manner. Before we back track and begin working on the website's layout and design, it's time to move into how to add products and what to do after orders come in!

Chapter 7. Adding a Product

Adding in products to your store is one of the most time-consuming parts of running an ecommerce business. Walking through the process isn't too terrible, but there are a lot of considerations, especially for someone that has never done it before.

Navigate to Product Page

Click "Products" on the navigation. At the bottom of the page is a link that will walk you through the entire section in a visual manner, and it is highly suggested that you take the time to review this.

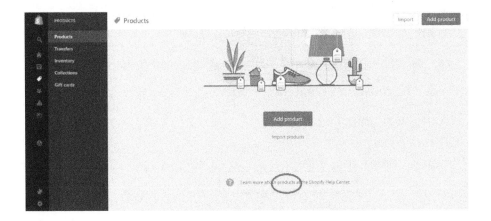

Add Product

Returning to the main product's page, you can click "Add Product" on the page or on the top bar.

The page that opens up will allow you to enter all of the information for your product.

Title

First, enter the title. Keep in mind that you will be able to setup variants of the same product, so if you're selling a t-shirt in multiple sizes or colors, then don't use the title to define these things. There's no reason to create a completely new product page for each color or variation of an item.

When entering your title, keep it concise and to the point. If it is appropriate, you can use the keywords you learned about during the market research stages to start your search engine optimization off on the right foot.

Description

The description should include a detailed account of your item. Again, you can utilize your keywords here. This is your chance to sell the item to the customer. If you have a great product with many interesting features, make sure to mention all of them. The better this section is written, the better you'll be able to make the sale.

Notice that the description textbox has options for optimizing the layout of your text. Take advantage of these text tools to bold fonts, add in bullet lists when it matters, and insert images and videos when they apply. Do not skimp on your description, but also don't over sell, or you'll run off potential customers.

Images

The images you add here are going to be the main images for your product. While you can add images directly to the product description, you also need to add them here in order to have the image displayed on your products pages that customers view; this is called the primary image.

Like descriptions, images are important, and it should never be skipped. Even digital products need some type of product image.

Pricing

Next, you'll price your product. You may notice that there is the option to include a "compare to" price. If you're offering a product at a reduced rate, make sure to note the suggested retail value here. Do not use this box as a means to create the illusion of a good deal where one doesn't exist; that's disingenuous and today's customers are smart enough to figure that out.

Inventory

If you're using barcodes and SKU numbers to track your inventory, you can input those here. If you're not, then you don't have to worry about them. Shopify will help track your inventory for you, so it is wise to use this if you're selling in large volumes.

Shipping

Enter the shipping information if it applies to your product. If it doesn't, then uncheck the box that says, "This item requires shipment."

For items that do require going through the post, take the time to weigh them in a box and with padding to get the actual shipping weight to enter here. By entering the weight of the box and shipping materials, the calculated shipping will be much more accurate, which helps you avoid losing money on shipping.

Variations

Here you'll setup the many variations available for this particular product. You'll notice that after you insert different variants, you'll be able to price each individually below, and remove certain variants if they don't apply.

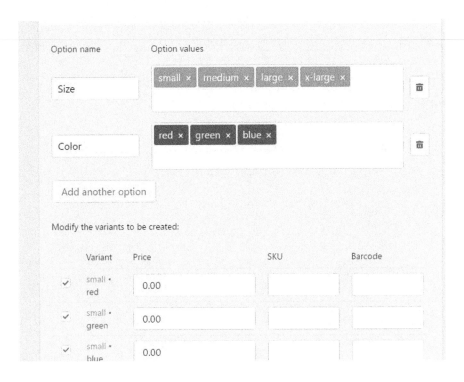

You will also notice that you can insert a separate barcode for each of these variants, making it easier to track your inventory and make sure you're not trying to sell an item you don't have in stock. You can always come back and edit these things later.

Search Engine Listing

At the bottom, you'll see the search engine listing editor, which allows you to take advantage of the way your products will appear in search engines should it get picked up during price comparisons or just within search results. It is ideal to shorten the URL, use keywords that are appropriately targeted to your audience, and keep things concise. Below is what this tool looks like. At this point, you will see a save button that can save your product information. But first, let's scroll back to the top.

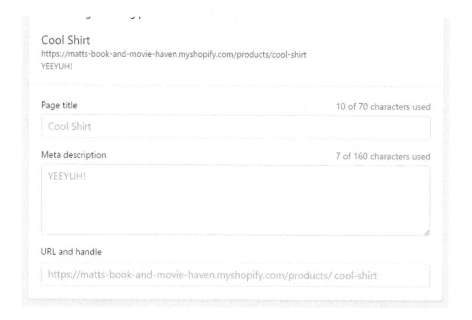

Sales Channels

Note that if you scroll back to the top before hitting save, you'll see a side bar on the right that includes two important items. The first is "Sales Channels," which is how you designate where the product will sell. This only works if you've taken the time to activate sales channels within your settings, and the amount of sales channels available is determined largely by the Shopify plan you're purchasing.

Organization

Beneath the "Sales Channel" box is the organization box that allows you to label your products in a way that makes it simple for you to navigate through your stock. This also helps customer's experience remain as streamlined as possible. Additionally, the tag section here is a great place to dump some of your keywords and group products together. Once you're done with both of these side-bar items, click the save button.

Import/Export Inventory

If you have a large inventory, you have the option of importing this data rather than taking the time to setup a product page for each item. This is advanced work for those that aren't familiar with spreadsheets, but if you have these skills, it can save a lot of time for high-volume sellers.

If you navigate to the top-right of the screen, you should see a little menu button next to the "Add Product" button. Clicking on this, you'll be given options to either export or import your inventory.

Exporting may be useful for other retail sites, checking that your inventory is correct, or getting an idea of what you have in stock.

To import a larger list of inventory rather than taking the time to setup each piece of every product, you can click "Import" from this dropdown menu.

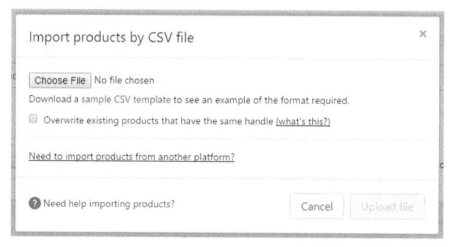

A dialog box will appear that gives you the option of uploading a CSV (comma separated value) file. It will also have a download link for a template so you can get yourself organized in a spreadsheet instead of trying to tick off all the boxes individually. You will also have an option to overwrite existing products through this method if something has changed or you've updated the description.

If you're comfortable with spreadsheets, download the sample template, and it'll save you time later if you are capable of being consistent while working within Excel. Just make sure to input all the information, and when it's possible, take the time to go review the product page for errors, add images, format text, etc.

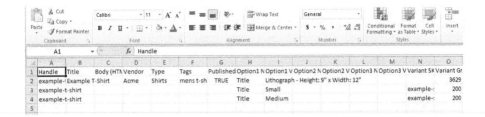

You can also import from other ecommerce setups, and Shopify will walk you through the process should you click on "import" and choose to do this. Another perk of the "export" option is that some platforms will accept and import the CSVs created by Shopify, making multiple-channels a lot easier to sell through.

Restock!

You'll become very familiar with the methods of stocking your store, especially as your business grows. Taking the time now to familiar yourself with it will make it much easier once you do have a large amount of a product to keep track of.

Now that we've setup our product, and we'll eventually repeat this for all of our products, it's time to consider our shipping methods.

Chapter 8. Shipping Methods

Unfortunately, if you're selling physical products, the work isn't over until the item is shipped to the customer, and the customer is happy. Taking the time to properly setup your shipping and getting yourself prepared for the shipping process will help you streamline the process a bit. The ideal situation is that you will offer as many shipping options as possible for customer to choose from. In this manner, they can receive items at the best prices or the most opportune times.

Manual Shipping Rates

Manual shipping rates are flat rates applied to each product. After setting a manual rate, the customer will immediately know the cost of shipping, and you can ultimately ship the product out in any manner you choose as long as it reaches the customer. I would try to mention the expected shipment times to help customers out.

The advantage of this method is that you don't have to weigh each item, but the disadvantages are plentiful. Not only are the customers not able to customize how they want an item shipped (what if they need it quicker?), but they may also be taken aback if your shipping charge is much higher than it needs to be. If customers order multiple items, your fixed rate may not take into account the size of the box required to ship them all at once. In general, it's not the best method to use.

The biggest disadvantage is that you may estimate poorly. Should the cost of shipping extend past the fixed rate you've set, then you will have to make up the cost difference on your own. This is fine if you build the price of shipping and materials into product prices, but you need to be diligent about how you price things.

If you only sell one line of product, and they're all practically the same size and weight, this option may be viable. If it isn't, you should offer shipping options to your customer.

Shopify USPS Shipping

Like eBay and PayPal, Shopify has a deal with the USPS that allows you to purchase labels at a discounted rate and print them off at home. Because you are most likely selling products that range from small to large, light to heavy, this is typically going to be the best method. All you need to do for your products is setup a weight, possibly slightly higher than the actual weight to accommodate for the packing materials and handling.

When the customer checks out, they can choose from several USPS options that allow them to pay more for quicker service. Shopify is automatically going to take the size and weight of your package into consideration and not allow them to order first-class mail when it's inappropriate, so there's no worries about getting underpaid for your shipping costs if your weights are correct. Additionally, the discounted rates (based on which tier of Shopify you use) will save you money. If you're a high-volume seller, and we all aim for that, then the Professional Plan's reduced rates will save you a healthy chunk of change over a period of time.

Other Carriers

You can also provide the option of other carriers for your customers, including UPS and FedEx, among others. Using the shipping setup in the settings, you'll be able to incorporate shipping APIs that allows these to be calculated much like the USPS costs are calculated. There is no discount involved with Shopify and these carriers, but if you have a business account with UPS, for example, your discount will still apply. Unfortunately, this is only available if you're a Professional member, which if you remember costs $299 per month. For high-volume sellers, it's worth having these additional options.

Fulfilment and Dropshipping

We've mentioned dropshipping briefly, but we'll cover this in greater detail later. This may be the best possible shipping method as the products aren't even in your possession or purchased by you until they are already sold to the customer!

There is also fulfilment shipping, which is similar in the idea that you're not the one handling the shipping, but unlike dropshipping, you already purchased the items, and now you're having them stored with a company that will ship them for you once they sell. This method may provide better profits than normal dropshipping, but you're still investing in the product and the fulfilment company's time. The ideal situation is to find a local fulfilment service where you can have products brought to without much fuss.

Shipping Settings

Now that we've covered the options for shipping, we have to actually go through the process of setting it up. We ran through this briefly during the "Settings" part of the Shopify interface, so you may already be familiar with this if you took the time to explore.

Navigate to your "Settings" page, and click on "Shipping."

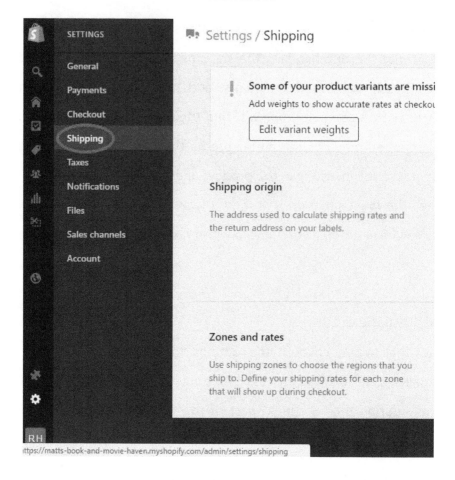

On this page, you'll see a number of things that you can adjust. This includes:

- Shipping Origin – This is the return address. Typically it will be your home address unless you have a dedicated business location. If you do not want your home address on the label, then you can always open a PO Box at your local post office to avoid this. Do not use a fake address.

- Zones and rates – Here you can setup your shipping zones and rates. This includes the ability to limit shipping to certain parts of the world. By default, everything is included, so it may be wise to adjust if you don't aim to offer international shipping. Within this section is how you setup manual shipping rates.

- Label format – Next, you'll see the label format section. If you're using special printers or labels, you can adjust this to fit your needs. If you're using a laser or inkjet printer that's pretty standard and just taping on labels, then leave it at the default.

- Packages – If you have a selection of boxes you use for your shipments, inserting these sizes will help minimize the amount of time inputting this information for products later.

- Additional Shipping Methods – This is where you setup methods other than calculated USPS rates.

Actually Shipping the Product

After an order is made, Shopify will notify you (unless you disabled notification), and they will give you the option to print out a shipping label. If you're using the standard calculated shipping, the label will default to match the information you've entered for calculated shipping. You can adjust this as needed. Always be sure your measurements and weights are correct.

To ship, you'll need a few things:

- **Boxes or bubble mailers** of multiple sizes that are appropriate for the products you stock. If you only have a few items for sale, you can hold off on buying in bulk, but once you begin moving product, you really need to keep some standard packaging materials on hand to speed up the process.

- **Padding**, such as bubble wrap and newspaper. Packing peanuts are becoming less common, and it is advised to avoid them as many customers find them inconsiderate to the environment.

- **Shipping tape**. Ideally, it will be clear. This way, if you're printing off paper labels and taping them to the box, you can tape over them a bit without it obstructing the information. Keep in mind that you're not supposed to tape over the barcodes. Nothing usually happens if you do, but it's technically discouraged by the USPS.

- **Printer** for printing labels.

- **Paper or label paper**. Label paper has adhesive back that means you can just peel and stick it to the box once it's printed.

Once a product is labeled, you can take it to the post office or you can login at USPS.com and schedule a pickup.

If working with third-party carriers, check with them to ensure you're following all their guidelines. These companies will almost always offer home pickup as well. If you're working with fulfilment services, Shopify and the service will help you set this up in a way that will automate the shipments thereafter.

No Rest for the Successful

That's all there is to shipping. It's not terribly complicated, but as your business grows, so does the workload involved. There will likely come a time when the workload of shipping starts to overshadow the very important work of market research, product listing, content generation, and marketing, etc. Once this happens, it may be time to bring on an employee or contractor, move to fulfilment services, or consider dropshipping. Let's talk about that.

Chapter 9. Dropshipping

We've mentioned dropshipping several times, but I've waited to explain this in any depth because I think it's important for first-time ecommerce entreprenuers to put in some of the work themselves at first. Not only are the profits slightly better per sale, but it gives you a great appreciation for how much work is involved in shipping products when sales are good. At some point, though, it becomes difficult to manage, especially if your goal is to remain a very small team rather than have a ton of employees.

Dropshipping eliminates the need to keep products in stock. Unlike simple fulfilment services, you don't even have to purchase anything ahead of time. Instead, you use dropshipping companies that offer the type of products you aim to sell to your market. When a customer purchases an item, the order is forwarded to the dropshipper, they take their cut for the cost of the product and service, and they ship it directly to the customer on your behalf. Since this keeps down overhead involved in purchasing stock, it opens your business up to sell many more products. While the return per sale is often lower than purchasing in bulk and selling, packaging, and shipping items on your own, the sheer amount of volume possible enables you to earn far greater income without working constantly, freeing you up to put time into content creation for product descriptions, blog posts, and marketing. It also means more time can be put into market and product research. For a large ecommerce business that isn't focused on selling branded products or producing their own products, this is hands down the best way to scale.

There are disadvantages to dropshipping, though. For starters, you are still the contact point for customer service concerns. Should an item arrive broken, you'll have to facilitate the refund, return, and replacement processes. Should your dropshipper send the wrong item, send a defective item, or otherwise mess up an order, it falls back on your business. For this reason, it is extremely important that you work with dropshippers you can trust. Additionally, it is paramount that you take the time to evaluate and test all the products you expect to sell through your Shopify store. Skipping the step of evaluating products is an easy way to get caught up in a downward spiral of selling low-quality goods. That is bad for your business, and it will hurt your reputation.

Additionally, it is much harder to keep track of what is in stock and out of stock. In the event that you're trying to sell a product that the dropshipping service no longer has in stock, or hasn't quite restocked, it can delay shipment or require you to cancel shipments because they cannot be fulfilled. This does not make for happy customers.

Because most people that use dropshipping as their ecommerce solution are going to diversify amongst several suppliers, it also becomes more difficult to track and log everything in an organized fashion. An additional concern with multiple sources of product is that a customer may order more than one product, and if all of those products come from different suppliers, they won't reach the customer at the same time. It adds to the cost of shipping because several shipments are made from each of these services, and thus lowers the amount you might have made per sale if you had your own warehouse and were able to ship these items as a single package.

Keeping good records is the key to ensuring everything is on the level, and being diligent about handling errors when they come up is going to help reduce the collateral damage of a poor customer experience. These concerns can be minimized by putting in the due diligence required to ensure your customer is getting a great product. Don't let simplicity of having a third-party (or several third parties) handle your products and shipments become your downfall. These disadvantages shouldn't scare you, as the overwhelming perks of not handling shipping, being able to sell larger quantities, and having a wider amount of products to choose from far outweigh these things if you can offer great customer service when issues arise.

How Dropshipping Works

Within Shopify, the dropshipping process is fairly simplified into three basic steps.

1. Customer orders a product from your store.
2. Shopify sends the order to you, and you send the order to the supplier. When possible, you can have the orders automatically forwarded to the dropshipper through apps or email notifications.
3. The dropshipper receives the order and ships the item to your customer.
4. The dropshipper notifies you that an item is shipped, and you notify Shopify, which then notifies the customer that the item is shipped.
5. Shopify lets the customer know when the item is out for delivery.
6. Shopify notifies you and the customer once the item is delivered.

There are ways to help automate this process, and in some cases, suppliers will even be willing to have access to your Shopify and fulfill these orders on your behalf.

Finding Dropshipping Services

There are number of companies that offer dropshipping services, and finding the ones that best fit your market means taking the time to look through many different sources. It is worth noting that a "dropshipper" is not a specific business model on its own. A dropshipper can be a wholesaler, a manufacturer, or even a retailer, and sometimes what business they're actually in can have an impact on the services they can provide for you. The goal is to avoid retailers, as their pricing is going to be significantly higher than wholesalers, and typically speaking, if you can work with a manufacturer that is also in the business of dropshipping, you'll get the best possible deals.

There are some "dropshippers" that aren't truly dropshippers at all. The tell-tale signs include:

- They charge you a monthly fee. The vast majority of dropshipping providers are not going to have monthly fees. While a fee of a few dollars per order isn't too uncommon, monthly charges are a red flag.

- They sell products openly. If they are selling products at retail to just anyone, they are probably not a legitimate dropshipping service. Most wholesalers are going to require that you have an account with them. It may just be a retail service that offers this as well, but there's little money to be made buying at full retail and selling at an inflated price.

It is also important to note that many businesses that offer dropshipping may have a minimum requirement for order amounts. This is often $500, but what if you're only selling smaller items one at a time from them? The best solution in these cases, especially if you truly want to work with them, is to contact their team and ask to pay $500 to put towards a credit that will come from your orders. This establishes trust and shows that you're not trying to waste their time. These types of investments can add up, but if you're truly doing your due diligence with product and market research, it will be worth it.

To actually locate these businesses, there are a number of resources available to you:

- **Contact manufacturers directly.** While most manufacturers are unlikely to offer this service for you, they will gladly give you a list of the wholesalers they work with. From there, you can contact the wholesalers that have the products you want. Repeat this process for a few manufacturers, and you'll start to notice some of the same names come up. These are going to be some of the best wholesalers to work with.

- **Search Google.** This method sounds like it should be extremely easy, but wholesalers, for some reason, don't put a lot of effort into marketing themselves. Normally, we'd assume the first page results are the best, but that may not be the case here. As bad as wholesalers are at promoting themselves, they are also horrible about having fancy websites. **In the case of dropshippers and wholesalers, do not assume that a bad looking website means a bad company**.

- **Lurk on the competition.** Who are your competitor's using? To find this out, try to locate your competitors that appear to be using dropshipping. Order a small package from them, and there's a good chance the supplier's return address will be on the package and not the company you actually purchased the item from. You can then Google this company to find out more about them.

- **Wholesale directories.** Many directories exist, and while many of them don't vet every entry, some do try to weed out the bad apples. You'll want to exercise due diligence when going this route, but you'll find many more leads than other methods. A few include:
  - http://worldwidebrands.com
  - http://salehoo.com
  - http://doba.com

- **Trade shows!** You may notice that finding dropshippers is basically the same process we discussed earlier about finding wholesalers. That's because many of these are the same companies, so it goes to reason that trade shows are also a good place to find dropshippers. Not only can you actually find people involved in supplying products, but you can ask others about their experience and look for leads that way.

Before Making Contact

Hopefully you haven't run out and started calling wholesalers and dropshippers just yet, because there are a few things you should handle before reaching out.

You should make sure your business is registered. You will most likely want to become an LLC even if you're essentially still a one-man team that's appropriate to call a sole proprietor. B2B (business-to-business) companies prefer to work with legitimate businesses. This helps improve your image to companies.

Along those same lines, you should also consider the fact that you're a new player in the industry. Do not overreach your position just yet. Build relationships, prove that you're a viable source of profit for these companies, and then you may be able to work out deals for better pricing and have the right to ask millions of questions.

Likewise, you'll want to have your Shopify store established for the best results. This is one of the reasons we waited so long to begin talking about dropshipping in any depth. While simply having your website setup with all the basic functions expected of a website is probably enough, it's better if you can demonstrate that you've been selling for at least a couple months. Doing these things first will ease the transition into dropshipping, and it encourages these companies to have faith that they're working with someone that's serious.

Choosing Products

At this stage, you should have a good idea of what your target market is, the niche your products fall into, and the level of quality you expect from your products. Ideally, these will be products that can easily demonstrate value through a simple video demonstration, product images, and descriptive writing.

After you locate a dropshipping service (or several) you'd like to utilize, it's time to dig through their products and find those that best fit your market and determine if they can sell at a profit. Keep in mind that you'll have to put in the effort to write great product descriptions. You cannot simply copy and paste the descriptions offered by the suppliers. This will often get flagged as unoriginal content by search engines and push your position on sites like Google so low that nobody ever finds your store organically. Truthfully, it's probably not going to be the best sales copy anyway, and it won't take into account the market you're selling to. Likewise, while you can utilize the images they have of their products, it is often smart to take the time to create your own if you have a decent camera and the know-how to take great images.

Once I find products I believe will be viable and can sell in amounts large enough to justify the work involved in creating the content required, I order a few of the item to test it out. During these tests, I ensure that the product meets the level of quality my customers expect. The reason I order more than one is to check that they are consistently manufactured products. Taking the time to test your dropshipped products will save you for making the blunder of selling a low-quality item. Additionally, having some hands-on experience makes it much easier to write blog posts, product descriptions, and marketing materials for these products.

For example, if I'm in the business of selling headphones, and I find two models I believe will be great, I'll order three of each. I'll test each product against itself three times. If the sound quality isn't consistent, I won't stock that product. If I like both products, I will also take the time to compare them against each other based on pricing, quality, aesthetics, and overall value. This is great for blog content, as comparison posts are highly popular content. This is especially useful if nobody else has handled a comparison on these two particular products. Once the product checks out, I take the time to take pictures, write descriptions, and possibly record a video demonstration. All of this content is aimed to help customers make a decision.

Even if you've sold 20 products from one dropshipper without ever running into quality issues, it is foolish to skip these steps. It only takes selling one faulty product to a handful of customers to drop your reputation. If a dropshipper consistently provides horrible products, it's safe to assume you should no longer attempt to work with them.

Choosing products can be difficult. As we discussed during the market research section, it is wise to take the time to find these products on other popular retail sites, read the reviews, and check their sales ranking. If a product has a sales rank on Amazon, for example, that exceeds 100,000, then it's probably not going to be easy to sell. Your market may allow for the sale of items that don't traditionally sell well on other platforms, but that will depend on your demographics, how you approach marketing, and your pricing.

Despite the challenges involved in choosing products to sell, the great news with dropshipping is that the time investment is much larger than the monetary investment. While "time is money" rings true, it also means that you won't have a hundred units sitting around should the item never sell for some reason. Ultimately, you can pull it from your Shopify store if it seems like it's just clogging up the product listings. The loss will be far less than if you were going the route of simply buying wholesale and attempting to sell them one at a time.

Do Your Research

Dropshipping has some intricacies that take you a step above a normal ecommerce seller with a small stock of items and a small market, but it's the best possible way to scale up your ecommerce business, especially once it becomes too much to handle all of the shipments. It's been repeated many times, but taking the time to handle some due diligence and research will help you avoid issues later. There are plenty of books and guides that promote the idea of setting up a dropshipping store in a few days' time, but the truth of the matter is that taking your time will net the best possible results if you've never went down this road before.

Expanding into dropshipping should ultimately be your goal if you're not producing digital products or your own line of products (either as manufacturer or through private label branding), and having a keen understanding of Shopify, the selling and shipping processes, and marketing efforts first ensures that you have a firm grasp on your business and the possible profits to be made.

Chapter 10: Customizing Your Shopify Store

Now that you understand your options as a new ecommerce entrepreneur, it's time to begin working towards creating a website, blog, and storefront worthy of the hard work you've put into finding products, suppliers, and understanding your market. The first step is customizing your Shopify store through the use of themes and putting together your pages.

Shopify Themes

One of the huge advantages of using Shopify for your ecommerce solution is that they offer a simple way to handle website and blog design. Not only are their themes attractive, but they also dramatically cut the costs involved in website design and hosting. Changing your Shopify theme is a simple process.

Start by going to your dashboard and clicking, "Online Store." This will give you a secondary navigation menu, but it will also open up the themes page by default.

From this page, you can customize the theme you have a chosen, and you can choose the way your website looks by choosing a new theme entirely. There are options for free themes, but you can also pay for themes. The route you go is entirely up to you; just keep in mind your target demographic. If you're at all unsure, you can take some screen shots of two different themes and run a survey (see the Marketing Research section) to garner opinions from potential customers.

Free themes and paid themes can be easily assessed by simply scrolling down on the page.

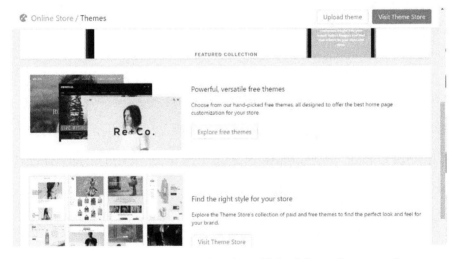

You'll notice that there are only a handful of free themes when you click the "Explore free themes" button. For our purposes, one of these will work fine for now, but we may wish to visit the theme store and actually purchase a design later on.

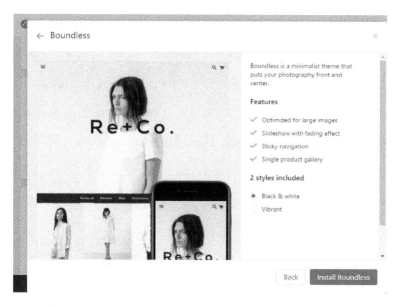

I like the "Boundless" theme from their list, so I've selected this. Shopify brings us to an overview of the theme, and I've decided it will work for my needs, so I'll click "Install Boundless."

After installing this theme, Shopify reminds me that I have yet to officially open my store. It can only be viewed with my password, but since I haven't finished setting up my customizations, I'll hold off on releasing it to the world for now.

For now, let's click "Customize theme." The page that shows up will have a list of options on the left-hand side, which will walk us through the process of customizing our website. This process is so easy that literally anybody can handle it.

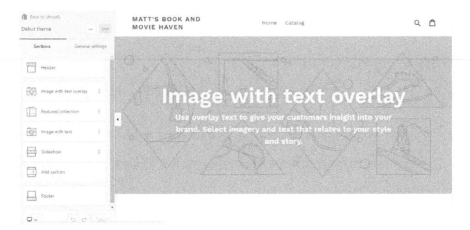

Once you've customized everything you currently can, you can save this and return later to make updates. Because the process is so simple, I won't bore you with a demonstration. Instead, let's begin putting together the pages all websites need to come across as legitimate.

Pages

Returning to your dashboard, we can access our pages by clicking on that "Online store" link once again and using the secondary navigation menu to choose "Pages."

Pages are static content. Unlike blog posts, these will always be linked on your website's navigation bar. These should be used for the most important pages of your website, but you can also use them for curated collections of products.

Every Great Website Has It...

There are some pages every site should have. These include:

- **Homepage**. This will simply link to your main storefront. You do not need to create this page as it's already incorporated into all themes on Shopify.

- **About Us**. This page should have a brief description of your business, when it started, staff (if you so choose), etc. It is wise to use this space to help solidify yourself as an authority in your niche. A sloppy "About Us" page says a lot about a business' credibility, especially a retail store.

- **Catalog**. This is your products page. This is also automatically generated by Shopify. However, you can create pages for specific categories/sales/etc. if you want. I'd limit this to one or two sections as the navigation menu will get clogged if you have too many pages linked on it.

- **Shipping**. This page should explain to customers how your shipping works. You do not need to tell them that your product is being dropshipped, but you do need to explain if you only ship in the US, if you offer shipping through third-parties, etc.

- **Returns**. This page should explain your return policy. It is advised to offer returns in most instances, but it is at your own discretion.

- **Contact**. Lastly, you need a page that includes a postal address, email address, and if you're able, a phone number. Having contact information available not only gives customers a way to reach out with issues, it also helps show the world that you're serious about your business and your customers.

Add a Page

To add a page, simply click "Add Page."

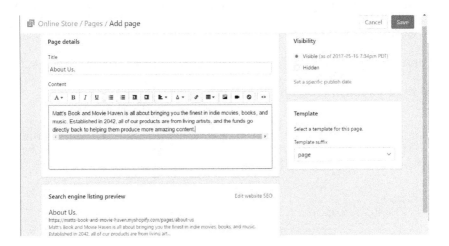

As you can see above, the new page feature works almost exactly like the product description tool. I've typed up a silly starting point, but you should take advantage of all the formatting tools, and don't forget to use the SEO editor to produce better search results. After we're finished, we can push, "Save."

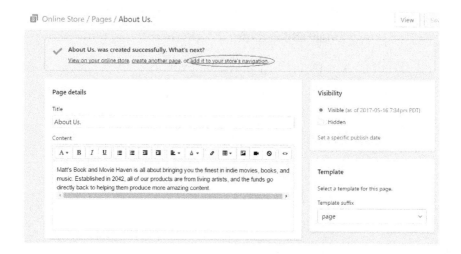

Shopify then notifies us that the page has been saved, and it gives us the option to either create another page or add it to your site's navigation bar. I'm going to go ahead and add this to our navigation, and then I'll finish creating the other pages.

Once you've created all your pages, let's go back to the "Online store" menu and choose "Navigation."

Navigation

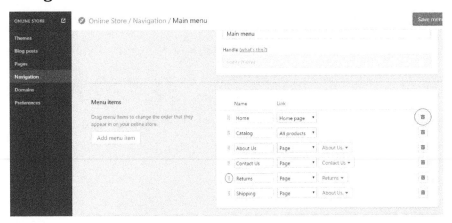

On the "Navigation" page, we'll be able to adjust a few details. First, if we haven't added all our pages, we can click "Add menu item" and select items from the lists. Second, we can rearrange the order of our menu links by clicking and dragging the dots to the left of each item we've added to our site. If you want to remove a link from the navigation, each item has a trash can symbol to the right of it. This won't delete the actual page, only the link on the menu. Once we're happy with our navigation menu, we can save it by pushing "Save." It's really that simple!

Blog Posts

Running a blog alongside your store is a smart way to help bring in additional traffic, highlight products you sell, and connect with your customers. Generally speaking, it is wise to keep a basic schedule for releasing posts. To make this easier, I like to write several blog posts in advance. From there, all I have to do is upload a new one if I'm not prepared to write another one to meet my publishing schedule. How often you post depends on preference and readership, but starting off with one or two posts each week is perfectly fine.

To add a blog to your site, you simply start by adding a blog post. This is once again in your "Online store" menu.

Once you're on the "Blog posts" page, just click "Create blog post" to get started. The setup on the page where you actually finish the blog post will be almost identical to the "Page" creation tool. Once again, you'll have the option of optimizing some SEO elements as well. When writing blog posts, optimizing for search engines is also ideal. Make sure to always include a primary image with your blog post, and the more images, the better.

Once your blog is created, make sure to go back to the "Navigation" page and add this to the navigation menu on your site!

Domains

A domain name is the .com, .net, .org, .etc address for your website. While Shopify gives your website a URL, having a domain name improves Search Engine Optimiation and makes your business look more legitimate to customers.

If you click on the "Domain" link from the "Online store" menu, you'll be given the option of purchasing a domain name or connecting a domain name you already own. Shopify charges $14 per year for a domain name, but this price includes WHOIS protection that keeps your information private, making it a very competitive rate within the domain registry industry. In the event that you've already purchased a domain name, you can choose "connect existing" instead.

When naming your domain, it should match your store's name as much as possible. Additionally, you can attempt to use the keywords you've researched to improve SEO slightly. There's no reason you can't link multiple domains to your website to help with this a bit, but it is generally best to advertise your site with a single domain name to help people remember it later.

Preferences

The last item in the "Online store" menu is "Preferences." This page has several important elements that you can customize.

- Homepage Title — This is what appears on the top of your web browser, and it has an impact on your search engine optimization and rankings. Typically, it should be the name of your store and possibly a few words based on what you sell. For example: "Matt's Video Game Haven — Retro Video Games, New Games, Customized Consoles."

- Meta description — As we've seen with product pages and other elements, the "meta description" is how search engines read your website. This should be a concise description of your store that utilizes your best performing keywords.

- Google Analytics — If you setup a Google Analytics account, you'll be able to copy/paste the code here to track visitors to your site. While Shopify does track some things, going this route can give you additional information about how people are finding your website, how long they stay, what links they click, etc.

- Facebook Pixel — Integrates Facebook Ads to help create Facebook Sponsored Posts.

- Password Page — When you open a store, it is put into password mode until you're actually ready to make it live. Alternatively, you can purposely have a password-only store. Here you can change that password, and you can also customize the message that customers see should they run into your store while it is password protected. If you haven't chosen a plan for Shopify yet, you cannot disable your password page.

Once you're done setting up your preference, you can click "Save," and that's all there is to it!

Additional Tools for Shopify

Now we're going to take the time to discuss a handful of some of the most useful apps and add-ons you can have for your ecommerce store. The great thing about many of these is that they don't cost anything extra!

To find apps, just navigate back to the main dashboard, and on the navigation menu, you'll see a link for "Apps" near the bottom.

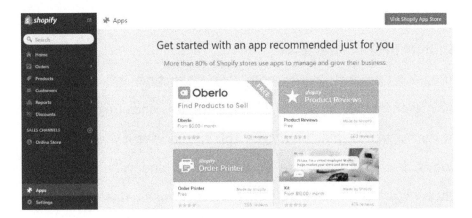

It starts by recommending some apps, but if you want to dig dipper, you can click the "Visit Shopify App Store" button on the top-right of the page. For now, let's discuss a few of these important recommended apps.

Oberlo

We mentioned this briefly before in the dropshipping section, but Oberlo is one of the easiest ways to import dropshipping items into your store. The app is completely free, easy to use, and many people have created dropshipping stores using only this service. The integration with Shopify means that Oberlo knows to ship items without you passing along order information! It also helps to reduce the likelihood of selling items that aren't actually available anymore. A huge business since 2015, Oberlo is quickly becoming Shopify's dropship entrepreneur's dream come true.

Shopify Product Reviews

Integrating product reviews onto your product pages is an excellent way to encourage buyers to interact, and it is encourages potential buyers to actually pull the trigger. This can backfire if you sell shoddy goods, but if you provide great products and service, you can encourage buyers to leave you positive product reviews. Shopify built this app, so it's a trusted method of handling this additional feature that most great stores include.

Shopify Order Printing

Simplifies all printing requirements associated with Shopify. A great tool when you rely on Shopify's shipping rather than going through third party carriers.

Boost Sales

Boost Sales costs $30/month, but it offers tools to easily create cross-sell and up-sell opportunities, loyalty programs that reward customers that purchase more, and other value-creating deals to help encourage sales. For high-volume sellers that utilize this app to its full potential, the cost is definitely worth trying it out.

Yottie

Yottie makes it painless to add YouTube videos throughout your site. While you can upload videos directly to Shopify, this makes any cross-marketing efforts with these videos easy, meaning you won't need to upload twice, the views increase on your YouTube videos, and customers can easily access content. The great thing is that Yottie is totally free.

Sales Pop

Sales Pop encourages customers to purchase other items by literally showing them what other people are purchasing in real time within your store. This works great for a site that has a decent amount of traffic. You will have to determine if this is practical for your demographic, as some may find it distracting or pushy, but in general, this simple free tool is an excellent way to boost sales.

Outfy

This intuitive app links together all of your social media outlets and allows you to post a product or advertisement to all of them with one click! While it isn't free, the low cost per posting is minimal considering the amount of time it saves someone that's utilizing many social media platforms. Give the free trial a whirl and decide if it's practical for your business.

Wishlist Plus

If you sell to a demographic that's likely to visit your store several times, integrating a wishlist mechanic may help boost sales, remind people of products they couldn't quite pull the trigger on, and eventually push that wish into a purchase. Wishlist Plus is free, and it makes it easy for customers to build a list of items they want to buy from you.

Amazon App

Shopify's Amazon app makes it incredibly simple to integrate your Shopify product listings on Amazon, creating additional sales channels. You will need to sign up for Amazon, and keep in mind that all Amazon seller fees still apply. Simplifying the process between multiple channels is always going to save you time, though.

Explore the App Store

Take some time to explore the app store once and awhile. There are countless tools that can help you customize the customer experience, expand your distribution, and simplify some of the many processes involved with running an ecommerce store. Many of the paid apps come with free trials, and the customer reviewers are active enough that you can gauge the usefulness of each app fairly quickly.

Always Customize

As you can see, customizing your store is simple, and Shopify's intuitive user interface makes it easy even if you're not highly skilled with technology. To help set yourself apart, be conscious of the way you customize the layout and design of your website. Have great logos created and integrate them into your store. Make sure your content is written well, formatted well, and easily accessible to your customers. Create a site that is tailored to your needs, and more importantly, tailored to your customer's needs.

Chapter 11: Search Engine Optimization

Search Engine Optimization (SEO) is an ever-evolving study and implementation of how to best make your website visible on search engines, especially Google. It is a highly involved topic, but a few key points can be applied to all of your content, whether that's your blogs, product descriptions, video descriptions on YouTube, social media posts, or any other faucet of your online presence. Knowing the basics will help you avoid common blunders that hurt your rankings. While the best approach to SEO is working with a professional, these tips will at least help you get started.

Content is King

Above all suggestions with SEO, the most important thing is that you are producing QUALITY content that is well written, proofread, and 100% original. Anything that isn't high quality is going to hurt you one way or another. Quality content is what builds trust in your name, and that high reputation will eventually translate to your positioning within search engines.

If you're not a great novelist, it may be imperative to have someone edit/proofread your work. If you know someone that will help, then by all means ask for their help. Offer to pay them back with your services, products, or even just money. If you don't know anyone, hiring a decent freelancer from sites like Upwork.com is suggested.

To ensure your original content isn't flagged a plagiarism, use CopyScape.com (or other plagiarism checkers), and scan your content 500 words at a time. This will let you know if there's anywhere else on the internet where the words you've written already exist verbatim. Avoid reusing manufacturer descriptions and pictures for this reason.

Again, no amount of SEO work matters if you don't produce excellent content. This is the most important thing you can do.

Implement Keywords

We already discussed the process of keyword research in the chapter about market research. If you haven't done this yet, I suggest that you go back and work your way through Google Keyword Tool as it is described there. Using that method, you should be able to create a relatively long list of keywords and order them from most likely to succeed to least important. As a rule of thumb, a high search count with a low competition is helpful.

I've suggested the implementation of keywords in many instances throughout the product description, blog, etc. As a rule of thumb, a keyword should not be utilized more than once per 100-200 words.

Stacking a keyword too many times on a single page can cause Google's algorithm to flag your site as spam.

Never implement keywords in a way that doesn't work organically. As your content must be quality, shoving in a keyword awkwardly just hurts your chances of sales even if it does happen to increase your rankings on Google.

Use your keywords in meta data fields, titles, your domain name if possible, and basically every spot you can. Even if you can only fit it in once, it is better to have it than not to have it.

You can write blog posts around your key words. Not only is this a good way to give yourself something to write about, but it ensures that you're using keywords in an organic and intelligent manner. Anyone can stack a page with keywords, but only great writers and smart SEO strategists can write a brilliant article around any given keyword.

Images and Video

Images and video, especially when they're original content, will greatly help with your search engine visibility. Not only does this help integrate your site into the Image and Video search features on Google, but it also gives you another chance to incorporate keywords within the alt-text and the video's description.

Back Links

Whenever possible, building relationships with folks that will gladly link to your store will help increase your search engine reach and general popularity in two ways. First, these links can drive traffic. Second, Google takes these types of links into account. The more legitimate sites that link to you site, the more legitimacy Google attributes to your site, pushing you a bit further up the search results. Linking from social media pages also helps.

Generating back links can be difficult work. Not all people want to post a link to someone's store, and many people in your niche are probably trying to make their own income. To help facilitate this, it may be wise to reach out to blogs that allow guest posts. With a guest post, you will write a blog post that is highly informative, fits within the constraints of the blogger you're working with, and contains only a small mention of your store, likely in a small biography at the end of the post. In this manner, you're not asking for a favor without offering something in return. Find a handful of blogs, and reach out to the folks running these pages. See if they'll link to your blog or store, and offer to do the same for them.

Create coupon codes and distribute them amongst the many free coupon and freebie websites. This not only encourages sales by offering a deal, but it also creates back links since your website will have to be linked in order for customers to enjoy the deal. These are some of the easiest links to build, but keep in mind that you only want these codes to appear on reputable websites.

Avoid creating back links the shady way. While it's possible to create links through spammy posts on blog comment sections, dumping content into directories, and paying for less-than-reputable services, these types of links may actually damage your search engine reputation more than they help, especially if you cannot be bothered to create new content. Coming back from horrible SEO decisions can be tough work, so just don't try these less-than-organic methods.

Local SEO

If you have a brick-and-mortar and your ecommerce is an extension of that, you can leverage some local SEO tricks by incorporating keywords revolving around the cities, counties, and states in the region you service the most. This is also true if you're seeing a large influx of sales from one region, even if you don't actually own a brick and mortar store. A simple example of this is using a keyword like, "Oxford RC Car Shop" instead of just "RC Car Shop." Because the "RC Car Shop" is still present, you're technically using that keyword as well. These long-tail, local keywords are especially useful in areas where businesses haven't quite caught on to smart practices for online marketing outside of paid advertisements and Facebook pages with only a few hundred subscribers.

Take the Plunge

If you can afford it, working with an SEO professional can be a huge help. You can find many SEO companies through a quick Google search, or you can use <u>Upwork.com</u> to find an individual freelancer to help you optimize your efforts. Keep in mind that you should only work with those that have a proven track record of producing results. Going for the cheapest option will very often net the least results. It is tempting to save money by hiring a cheap freelancer from overseas, but it may not be in your best interest at the end of the day.

If you cannot afford a great SEO professional, your other option is to put in the time to learn the LATEST SEO methods. Avoid anything labeled as "black hat," and keep in mind that articles from 2012 may not be as relevant to 2017 as they seem. Other than the fact that content will always be king and reputation matters, SEO is ever-evolving, and keeping up-to-date is half the battle with great visibility inside of search engines.

Chapter 12: Seizing an Opportunity

All of your product research and learning about and connecting with your target market is going to come in handy on a day-to-day basis, but it is important to pay attention to what is coming ahead as well. Considering this, holidays and trending topics can be exactly what you need for a boost in sales. While these are not always long-term investments, they can be highly profitable short-term investments.

Holiday Sales

As a seller, you should be excited when holiday seasons come around. This applies to most niches, and even if you put almost no effort into creating sales and changing the user experience for these events, you will likely see a boost in sales during the "holiday season."

The great thing is that ecommerce sales are increasing every year as more people stay online and avoid the lines while finding better deals. Leveraging this to your advantage is generally pretty easy. Not only can you setup sales, but you can send out coupon codes to your mailing list as a holiday treat, market holiday-specific items (if they fit your niche), and create amazing package deals just for the season.

The trick to getting the most out of holiday sales is to prepare ahead of time. Being well prepared to launch your holiday-based efforts before November stars will make it easier to get the most out of the season. Not only should you prepare for Black Friday and Cyber Monday sales (even if they're just coupon/promo codes), but you should also prepare for Christmas, post-Christmas, and New Year's sales. This is the season of heavy spending, and being prepared ahead of time makes it easy for you to capitalize.

As part of your effort to prepare, altering your website copy to fit the season is a great way to make it clear that you're all about the holiday spirit. Being somewhat politically correct may help in certain demographics, but more importantly, changing your website copy is a chance to insert many holiday-centric keywords. This is a great time to be writing blogs about "Top 10 Christmas Gifts for RC Car Enthusiasts in 2017," and it's a great time to curate collections on your Shopify store that are specifically aimed at certain members of the family, spouses, etc.

Taking full advantage of the holiday season by rolling out a festive, sale-ridden campaign may just be the first-year boost you need to justify continuing your business! Do not underestimate this opportunity. Some businesses see more than half of their income from the November-January period.

Spotting Trends

The best way to spot trends is to hang out where your target demographic hangs out, whether that's online on "in real life." If you pay attention to your customer, you will see what your customer likes, what is growing within the social circles of your customers, and you'll be able to take advantage of this by providing them a solution to their needs or wants.

Not only can you learn about new products, but this also expands into how to keep your blog relevant. If there's an ongoing debate within your demographic about the usefulness of celestial navigation (or anything), then you should weigh in on this through your blog, and then propagate that blog through your social media outlets.

If something catches your eye as a growing trend amongst your customer base, take the time to give it a bit of research. Search those popular hangouts your customer frequent. Ask your social media followers a couple questions. Handle some keyword research and see if keywords associated with these apparent trends have been growing in the last few months. Look at a competitor that you know is on top of their game. The better you understand what is happening within your market, the easier it is to keep relevant. Even if the trend dies off shortly, a smart campaign with products that fit these trends can be a boost in sales that makes it possible to expand just a bit further.

Listen to Your Customer

Past trends and holiday sales that are fleeting, there are going to be developments in your niche that you need to keep on top of. The easiest way to accomplish this is to remain in constant contact with your market demographic. In an ideal situation, the niche or market you cater to will be something that personally interests you. This may not always be the case, but if it is, you are probably already on top of these things. If you aren't part of the same demographic, you need to act as if you were. This doesn't mean literally trying to emulate anybody, but you need to frequent the same websites, watch the same YouTube videos, and join the same Facebook groups. If a development within your niche happens and you fail to respond to it somehow, you're going to get left behind. In some instances, this can be a new product that everyone wants. In others, it may be that there's an opening for a specific type of product to solve some type of need. Listen to your customers always.

Likewise, if customers hate a product you're selling, it's time to quit selling it. This is one of the reasons you want to use product review apps in your store. It encourages input from those that can best guide you to meet your target market's desires. The more you listen, the better you will be at meeting your customer's before they even reach the middle.

Conclusion

Congratulations. You have set your eyes on an amazing business opportunity that can easily replace your nine-to-five job if you're just willing to put in the hard work, take time to research, and have a little bit of capital to spare. Ecommerce can be honest work, and it's an exciting, ever-evolving adventure to run your own online store, blog, and website. With the knowledge you have accumulated, you should be well on your way to success!

CPSIA information can be obtained
at www.ICGtesting.com
Printed in the USA
LVHW050019090519
617203LV00010B/257/P

9 781547 084432